WICKED WOMEN

WICKED WOMEN

Notorious, Mischievous, and Wayward Ladies

from the Old West

CHRIS ENSS

TWODOT®

GUILFORD, CONNECTICUT
HELENA, MONTANA

A · TWODOT® · BOOK

An imprint and registered trademark of Rowman & Littlefield

Distributed by NATIONAL BOOK NETWORK

British Library Cataloguing-in-Publication Information available

Library of Congress Cataloging-in-Publication Data available

ISBN 978-1-4930-0801-8 (paperback)
ISBN 978-1-4930-1392-0 (e-book)

♾™ The paper used in this publication meets the minimum requirements of American National Standard for Information Sciences—Permanence of Paper for Printed Library Materials, ANSI/NISO Z39.48-1992.

For Big Nose Kate, who gave as good as she got from Doc Holliday

Contents

Acknowledgments

Chasing down the history of the wicked women of America's Old West has been a daunting but rewarding task. I have depended constantly upon the historians and photo archivists from Maine to Montana to complete this volume.

I am sincerely grateful to Chrystal Carpenter Burke at the Arizona Historical Society for going out of her way to provide me with some of the rarely seen pictures of the lady gamblers included in this volume. The Historical Society of New Mexico and the State Records Center and Archives department in Santa Fe were most helpful in supplying much of the information needed to write about Gertrudis Maria Barceló. The staff at the California History Room in Sacramento is always attentive and kind and makes visiting the library a true joy.

I appreciate the assistance of Jerry Bryant at the Adams Museum and House in Deadwood, South Dakota, and that of Matthew Reitzal at the South Dakota State Historical Society. Special thanks to Sara Keckeisen at the Kansas State Historical Society in Topeka for generously giving her time and research talent as well.

The historians at the Nevada County Historical Library and Searls Library helped locate records on Eleanora Dumont and Texas Tommy. The staff members at each of the aforementioned locations were generous with their time and extremely patient. Their assistance is greatly appreciated.

Thanks most especially to my brilliant editor, Erin Turner. I'm much obliged for all you've done over the years.

Introduction

The effect of vice upon the destiny of the expanding western frontier was considered by some religious and political leaders in the mid-1850s to be a sign of a rotten and decaying civilization. In 1856 Methodist pastor John M. Chivington told a congregation in Nebraska that "the extravagant development of immorality, particularly the development of immoral women given to gambling, whiskey drinking and prostitution, marks the decadence of a potentially great nation." Ernest A. Bell, the secretary of the Illinois Vigilance Association, maintained that "from the day the serpent lured the first woman in the garden there have been few days and nights when some daughter of Eve's has not been deceived into a wicked life by some serpent or other. It has not changed and will not change."

In 1849 women of easy virtue found wicked lives west of the Mississippi when they followed fortune hunters seeking gold and land in an unsettled territory. Prostitutes and female gamblers hoped to capitalize on the vices of the intrepid pioneers.

According to records at the California State Historical Library, more than half of the working women in the West during the 1870s were prostitutes. At that time madams—those women who owned, managed, and maintained brothels—were generally the only women out west who appeared to be in control of their own destinies. For that reason alone, the prospect of a career in the "oldest profession" must have seemed promising—at least at the outset.

Often referred to as "sporting women" and "soiled doves," prostitutes generally ranged in age from seventeen to twenty-five, although girls as young as fourteen were sometimes hired. Women over twenty-eight years of age were generally considered too old to be prostitutes.

Rarely, if ever, did working women use their real names. To avoid trouble with the law as they traveled from town to town and to protect their true identities, many of these women adopted colorful new handles like Contrary Mary, Little Gold Dollar, Lazy Kate, and Honolulu Nell.

The vicinities in which their businesses were located were also given distinctive names. Bordellos and parlor houses typically thrived in the part of a city known as "the half world," "the badlands," "the tenderloin," "the twilight zone," or "the red-light district."

The term "red-light district" originated in Kansas. As a way of discouraging would-be intruders, brazen railroad workers around Dodge City began hanging their red brakemen's lanterns outside their doors as a signal that they were in the company of a lady of the evening. The colorful custom was quickly adopted by many ladies and their madams.

Generally speaking, a prostitute's class was determined by her location and her clientele. High-priced prostitutes plied their trade in parlor houses. These immense, beautiful homes were well furnished and lavishly decorated. The women who worked at such posh houses were impeccably dressed, pampered by personal maids, and protected by the ambitious madams who managed the business. In general, parlor houses were very profitable. Madams kept repeat customers interested by importing women from France, Russia, England, and the East Coast of the United States. These ladies could earn more than $25 a night. The madams received a substantial portion of the proceeds, which were often used to improve the parlor house or to purchase similar houses.

The lifestyle was, without a doubt, a dangerous one, and many women despised being a part of the underworld profession. As Nebraska madam and prostitute Josie Washburn noted in 1896: "We are there because we must have bread. The man is there because he must have pleasure; he has no other necessity for being there; true if we were not there the men would not come. But we are not permitted to be anywhere else."

Entertaining numerous men often resulted in assault, unwanted pregnancies, venereal disease, and even death. Some prostitutes escaped the hell of the trade by committing suicide. Some drank themselves to death; others overdosed on laudanum. Botched abortions, syphilis, and other diseases claimed many of their lives as well.

In the late 1860s a concern for the physical condition of prostitutes—and moreover, for the effect their poor health was having on the community at large—was finally addressed. Government officials, alerted to the spread of infectious illnesses, decided to take action against women of ill repute. At a public meeting in New York City, a bill was introduced that aimed to curtail the activities of prostitutes who did not pass health exams. The goal of the bill was to stop the advance of what morally upright citizens termed the "social evil."

A March 14, 1867, *New York Times* article reported on the proceedings:

> *The committee on public health today reported Mr. Jacob's bill for further suppression of prostitution. It was amended, at the suggestion of the author, by providing for the medical inspection of all females in registered houses and the detention of those diseased in a retreat under the control of the Board of Health.*
>
> *During the morning large numbers of persons representing the houses of ill fame congregated in the cloak room, bitterly opposing the bill and attempting to smother it. But Dr. Jacob and his associates on the committee stood firm and reported the bill. It will be pushed forward at the earliest possible moment. It provides a heavy penalty upon all persons who let and keep houses for unlawful purposes, of the description named, the penalties being a lien upon the property. The Police Commissioners are directed to cause a registration to be made of all houses of prostitution and of the inmates in them. The Board of Health is directed to make thorough periodical sanitary inspections of the registered places and to remove all diseased persons in them to a "retreat," which they are directed to provide.*
>
> *The bill receives the endorsement of both the police and health authorities. Another bill has been introduced and is now before the committee on state charitable institutions, which proposes to license the houses, and appoint a commission for that purpose. This measure, it is understood, is backed by the parties interested in the business of prostitution and is not likely to be favorably considered.*

As time went on, houses of ill repute and the prostitutes who worked in them came under constant attack from outraged citizens who insisted the brothels be shut down. Madams hired police to protect their girls and their businesses from forced closures by private citizens. Having such safety measures in place cost madams an initiation fee of $300 to $500. The monthly payment for continued support was $30 to $50. Additionally, expensive fines—ranging from $750 to $900 an offense—were levied against madams who operated houses without a license.

Although prostitution was far from being socially acceptable, it was viewed by many as a necessary evil. The profession was tolerated for two important reasons. First, the public believed it prevented randy cowboys and miners from raping decent women. Second, given that new mothers were expected to refrain from having sex while breastfeeding—and those children were not completely weaned until they were two years old—it was commonly accepted that husbands in such situations often sought satisfaction in the arms of ladies of easy virtue.

Still, prostitutes and madams were criticized and looked down upon by "God-fearing" men and women who were infiltrating the West in ever-increasing numbers. A few brave souls dared to defend the "fallen angels," chastising those who passed judgment on them. Some even had poems published in local newspapers expressing their thoughts on the matter. One such defender was miner John Brantingham, whose verses appeared in a 1901 Colorado newspaper. His words expressed the feelings of many citizens who benefited from the benevolence of the women of ill fame: "There is so much bad in the best of us and so much good in the worst of us. That it hardly behooves any of us to talk about the rest of us."

Despite the moral objections to prostitution, madams and their entourages were often greeted with shouts of joy when they first arrived in mining camps. Their presence in the sparsely populated West was cause for celebration among many pioneer men. "Public women" performed a variety of services for lonely men, and, in the absence of the men's wives, they offered much-needed comfort and companionship. It was not unusual for these shady ladies to be treated as friends and confidants by their customers.

Fallen women learned to live with the negative social stigma associated with their trade. They survived the rough, lawless men in their company and the gossip of "God-fearing" women, and strongly defended themselves whenever the occasion arose.

Washburn chose to stand up to critics of her profession in a series of published articles. She blasted the hypocrisy of politicians who sought to eliminate prostitution while continuing to patronize parlor houses. Dodge City's Squirrel Tooth Alice used a revolver instead of a pen to ward off violent, hotheaded patrons. Madam Rose Ellis of Grass Valley, California, was always armed but decided to battle the residents who thought she was evil incarnate by giving generously to the poor in the community.

The picture of the early American West would not be complete without the image of a fashionably dressed madam standing at the top of saloon stairs and surveying the activity below. All eyes watched as she stepped down into her domain to make sure the women in her care were showing clients a good time. Some madams would entertain customers by dealing a hand of poker, but that job was often reserved for those ladies who were professional cardsharps.

The life of a professional gambler was unsettling and speculative. Most gamblers rode the circuit with the seasons. In the summer the big play was in the northern mining camps, and during the winter the southern towns provided the richest activity. Women gamblers were a rarity, and the most successful lady gamblers possessed stunning good looks that helped disarm aggressive opponents and gave them something pretty to admire as they lost their money.

Throughout the history of the early gaming days of the Old West, women proved they were just as capable as men at dealing cards and throwing dice, and they brought both pleasure and heartache to the miners of the gold and silver camps. Lady gamblers such as Eleanora Dumont saw themselves simply as businesswomen with a talent to offer the public. Players flocked to Madame Dumont's entertainments, their money drawn from their pockets as they indulged in their all-absorbing passion for games of chance. Gertrudis Maria Barceló owned her own gambling house in Santa Fe, New Mexico, where she catered to the rich and sophisticated in her pristine establishment. Cardsharps such as Kitty LeRoy flitted from Texas to California and South Dakota, dealing hands at rowdy saloons from El Paso to Deadwood. The gambling den LeRoy eventually owned was well known for the violence of its patrons, one of whom shot and killed her.

The lives and careers of a number of lady gamblers were cut short either at the mercy of a cowboy who resented losing to a woman or by their own hand. Legendary Belle Starr was gunned down by an unknown assailant some historians speculate was a riverboat gambler she humiliated at the poker table. Colorado cardsharp Minnie Smith found life dealing blackjack to be unbearably lonely and killed herself at the age of forty-five.

Cardsharps were looked down upon by polite, upstanding citizens, as was gambling as a whole. The women who specifically ran gambling parlors were accused of being many things, including thieves, home wreckers, and prostitutes. Along with roulette, craps, and poker, their activities were noted as the chief reason for the downfall of morality. By 1860 the games of faro and roulette were banned in California. Gamblers, both male and female, were being forced out of the "profession."

At one time or another, all the women included in this volume were living on the fringes of the law. Civic groups opposing gambling on moral grounds fought to make it illegal. Those high rollers in ball gowns who refused to comply with the law found creative ways to keep the bets alive. Belle Siddons conducted business from inside an oversize wagon that could be moved whenever the authorities came near. Belle Cora disguised her illegal activities to look like simple neighborhood parities. Alice Ivers, better known as Poker Alice, took up the profession in 1865 and continued in the business for more than sixty years. Government mandates against gambling did not stop the notorious faro dealer from playing the game. She died broke at the age of seventy-nine. "I gambled away fortunes," she once told a friend, "but I had a ball doing it."

Whether they were throwing dice or shuffling cards, enterprising women bet on their own gambling talents and secured a place for themselves in Old West history. Notable female gamblers were few in number, but they left an indelible mark on the history of the Old West. Soiled doves left their mark as well. *Wicked Women: Notorious, Mischievous, and Wayward Ladies from the Old West* examines the stories of these resourceful but much-maligned women whose combined adventures offer a colorful and often-overlooked portrait of the early days of the West.

Libby Thompson

Squirrel Tooth Alice

"She wasn't a coward; she wasn't a weakling; and she sure wasn't average."

THELMA THOMPSON WILSON, SQUIRREL TOOTH ALICE'S
GREAT-GRANDDAUGHTER, 1999

Libby Thompson twirled gracefully around the dance floor of the Sweet-water Saloon in Sweetwater, Texas. A banjo and piano player performed a clumsy rendition of the house favorite, "Sweet Betsy from Pike." Libby made a valiant effort to match her talent with the musician's limited skills. The rough crowd around her was not interested in the out-of-tune playing; their eyes were fixed on the billowing folds of her flaming-red costume. The rowdy men hoped to catch a peek at Libby's shapely, bare legs underneath the yards of fabric on her skirt. Libby was careful to let them see only enough to keep them interested.

Many of the cowboy customers were spattered with alkali dust, grease, or plain dirt. They stretched their eager, unkempt hands out to touch Libby as she pranced by, but she managed to avoid all contact. At the end of the performance, she was showered with applause, cheers, and requests to see more. Libby was not in an obliging mood. She smiled, bowed, and hurried past the enthusiastic audience as she made her way to the bar for a drink.

A surly bartender served her a glass of apple whiskey, and she headed off to the back of the room with her beverage. When she wasn't entertaining patrons, Libby could be found at her usual corner spot by the stairs. A large, purple velvet chair waited for her there along with her pets, a pair of prairie dogs. As Libby walked through the mass of people to her spot, she saw three grimy, bearded men surrounding her seat. One of the inebriated cowhands was poking at her animals with a long stick.

"Boys, I'd thank you kindly to stop that," she warned the unruly trio. The men turned to see who was speaking, then broke into a hearty laugh once they saw her. Ignoring the dancer they resumed their harassment of the small dogs. The animals batted the stick back as it neared them, and each time the men would erupt with laughter.

Libby watched the three for a few moments, then slowly reached into her drawstring purse and removed a pistol. Pointing the gun at the men, she said, "Don't make me ask you again." The drunken cowhands turned to face Libby, and she aimed her pistol at the head of the man with the stick. Laughing, the man told her to "go to hell." "I'm on my way," she responded, pulling the hammer back on the gun. "But I don't mind sending you there first so you can warn them," she added. The cowboy dropped the stick, and he and his friends backed away from Libby's chair. One by one they staggered out of the saloon. Libby put the gun back into her purse, scooped up her frightened pets, scratched their heads, and kissed them repeatedly.

Libby Thompson was known by most as Squirrel Tooth Alice. Named for a slight imperfection in her teeth and for the burrowing rodents she kept that were often mistaken for squirrels, Alice was one of the most famous madams on the western front.

Libby Thompson was born Mary Elizabeth Haley on October 18, 1855, in Belton, Texas. Her parents, James Haley and Mary Raybourne, owned a plantation along the Brazos River. Prior to the Civil War, the Haleys were a wealthy family. Libby, along with her three brothers and two sisters, was accustomed to the finer things in life. When the South lost the war, the Haley fortune went with it. James managed to hold on to his land, and his children helped him work the rich soil. He was never a big success as a farmer, but he did manage to keep his family fed. He was not able to protect them from hostile Indian parties that raided home-steads and stole their livestock, however.

In 1864 Comanche Indians raided the Haley plantation and took Libby captive. James and Mary searched for their daughter for three years. After locating the tribe that had taken Libby, they learned that a ransom was demanded for her release. The distraught Haleys agreed to pay the price, and Libby returned home in the winter of 1867.

Speculations as to how the Comanche Indians treated female captives ranged from forcible rape and torture to marriage and servitude. Libby rarely spoke of the harrowing ordeal. Historians at the University of Texas note her behavior was indicative of most captives. Even if she had described the perilous ordeal to the curious Belton population, it would not have changed the way they treated her. Libby showed no physical signs of abuse, and the public took that to mean she willingly submitted to the Indians' demands. Libby was shunned from polite society and ostracized from the community.

Rejected by friends, neighbors, and some family members, Libby was driven to keep company with an older man who accepted her in spite of her experience with the Comanche Indians. When Libby brought the gentleman friend home to meet her parents, she introduced him as her husband. James was so enraged at the idea of his teenage daughter being taken advantage of, he shot and killed Libby's lover. The scandal further tarnished her already questionable reputation.

At the age of fourteen, Libby ran away from home to start life fresh in a new location. She chose Abilene, Kansas, as the spot to begin again. She took a job as a dance hall girl in one of the town's many wild saloons. It was in one of these establishments that she met a cowboy gambler named Billy Thompson. Billy was ten years older than Libby. He swept her off her feet with his boyish good looks, irresistible charm, and promise of an exciting life on the frontier. The two left Abilene together in 1870 and made way for Texas.

When Libby wasn't following her man over the Chisholm Trail while he punched cows for any cattle drive crew that needed him, the pair was holed up in a saloon. Billy would gamble, and Libby would dance. Dance hall girls were paid well and could earn even more if they engaged in acts of prostitution. Libby was not opposed to entertaining gentlemen in that manner if it brought in extra cash. As long as she shared her income with Billy, he didn't object, either. The carefree couple drifted from town to town, staying long enough to tire of each place and then moving on.

In 1872 Libby and Billy left Texas and headed back to Kansas. This time they settled in Ellsworth. Work was readily available there. Numerous cattle drives came through the area, and there was a lot of money to be made and won at the busy saloons. In less than six months, Libby and Billy had amassed a small fortune. Most of the pair's wealth was lost after a few luckless nights of gambling. By this time Libby was expecting their first child. Broke and desperate, Billy decided to join a drive heading south.

Cohabitation without the benefit of marriage was illegal in the Old West, so Libby and Billy lied about their marital status. They did so not only to get away with living together but also for Libby to go along on the cattle drives. As trail boss Billy was permitted to have his family accompany him. Holed up in the back of a wagon, a pregnant Libby followed the herd from Kansas to Oklahoma. On April 1, 1873, she gave birth to a son and named him Rance. Three months later, in a formal setting, Billy decided to legally marry the mother of his child.

The Thompsons were vagabonds; it was not in their natures to lay down roots, and even having a son did not inspire the couple to settle down. They wanted nothing more than to drift freely from cow town to cow town plying their individual trades. A deadly, impulsive act ultimately robbed them of their uninhibited, wandering lifestyle.

On August 15, 1873, after an all-night drinking spree, Billy accidentally shot and killed a Kansas sheriff. He was arrested, and the cattle company he worked for bailed him out of jail. Worrying about reprisals from the sheriff's friends and family and fearing for their lives, Billy and Libby took Rance and ran from the cow town. Their itinerant lifestyle then became a matter of necessity rather than choice.

Libby and Billy sought refuge from the law in Dodge City. Libby found work as a dancer, madam, and part-time prostitute. Billy gambled at the saloons around town. They befriended some of the area's most famous residents, namely Wyatt Earp and his lover, Mattie Blaylock. After Kansas the Thompsons traveled to Colorado and then back to Texas. Along the way Libby gave birth to three more children. One of those children died from fever.

By the summer of 1876, Libby and her family were settled in Sweetwater. She and Billy purchased a small ranch outside town and a dance hall on Main Street. Libby was the main attraction on stage, but the stable of women who worked for her behind the scenes brought in the lion's

Libby Thompson was one of the most popular prostitutes and dance hall girls in Dodge City, Kansas. She was rarely seen without her pet prairie dogs, which many mistook for squirrels.

share of the business. Billy protected his wife whenever he needed to but spent much of his time away from the saloon, leaving the daily operations of the brothel and tavern to Libby.

Libby was not shy or ashamed of how she earned a living. She openly confessed her profession to anyone who asked. When the census was taken in the area, she boldly listed her occupation as "one who diddles and squirms in the dark." Libby's frankness drew customers to her place, but that wasn't the only reason. Her pet "squirrels" also garnered a lot of attention. The prairie dogs were good pets. She took the small animals with her wherever she went.

Early in their relationship, Billy accepted and encouraged his wife's profession. In later years, however, it was a source of tension between the two. Billy's absence while on long cattle drives took its toll on the marriage as well. Both began to look to other people to make them happy and fill the voids. Each had a succession of lovers, but they never lost the connection that initially brought them together. They always found their way back to each other. During the course of their twenty-four years of marriage, the couple had nine children. History recorded that Billy was absent for much of their children's upbringing.

In 1896 Billy returned to Sweetwater after having spent several months in Colorado gambling. During his stay in Cripple Creek, Colorado, he contracted consumption. When he arrived in Texas, he was dying from the disease. Libby was unable to provide adequate care for her husband, so she sent him to his family in southern Texas. Billy passed away on September 6, 1887, at the St. Joseph Infirmary in Houston.

Libby didn't stay single for long. She moved in with a man simply known as Mr. Young. Young was a cattle rustler who'd had several run-ins with the law. Historians suspect that Mr. Young—not Billy Thompson— was the father of Libby's ninth child, contrary to what she had led her late husband to believe. Regardless, Mr. Young proved to be just as bad at parenthood as Billy. Libby was lacking in that department as well. In addition to the nine children she had with Billy, and possibly Mr. Young, she had three more children with two different men. Several of her sons chose a life of crime, and many of her daughters followed her into the prostitution trade.

Libby's days as a madam came to an end in 1921. She retired at the age of sixty-six and lived with her children on an alternating basis. The last month of her life was spent at the Sunbeam Rest Home in Los Angeles. Squirrel Tooth Alice died of natural causes on April 13, 1953. She was ninety-seven years old.

Kitty LeRoy

The Deadly Paramour

"Spirits of the good, the fair and beautiful, guard us through the dreamy hours. Kinder ones, but, perhaps less dutiful, keep the places that once were ours."

POETIC EDITORIAL IN MEMORY OF THE SLAIN KITTY LEROY
FROM THE *BLACK HILLS DAILY TIMES*, 1883

A grim-faced bartender led a pair of sheriff's deputies up the stairs of Deadwood's Lone Star Saloon to the two lifeless bodies sprawled on the floor. One of the deceased individuals was a gambler named Kitty LeRoy, and the other was her estranged husband, Sam Curley.

The quiet expression on Kitty's face gave no indication that her death had been a violent one. She was lying on her back with her eyes closed and, if not for the bullet hole in her chest, would simply have looked as though she were sleeping. Sam's dead form was a mass of blood and tissue. He was lying faceup with pieces of his skull protruding from a self-inflicted gunshot wound. In his right hand he still held the pistol that had brought about the tragic scene.

For those townspeople who knew the flamboyant twenty-eight-year-old LeRoy, her furious demise did not come as a surprise. She was a voluptuous beauty who used her striking good looks to take advantage of infatuated men who believed her charm and talent surpassed any they'd ever known.

Nothing is known of her early years: where and the exact date she was born, who her parents and siblings were, or what she was like as a child. The earliest historical account of the entertainer, card player, and sometime soiled dove lists her as a dancer in Dallas, Texas, in 1875. She was a regular performer at Johnny Thompson's Variety Theatre. She had dark, striking features; brown, curly hair; and a trim, shapely figure. She dressed in elaborate gypsy-style garments and always wore a pair of spectacular diamond earrings.

Kitty's nightly performances attracted many cowboys and trail hands. She received standing ovations after every jig and shouts from the audience for an encore. The one thing Kitty was better at than dancing was gambling. She was a savvy faro dealer and poker player. Men fought one another—sometimes to death—for a chance to sit opposite her and play a game or two.

In early 1876, after becoming romantically involved with a persistent saloonkeeper, Kitty decided to leave Texas and travel with her lover to San Francisco. Their stay in Northern California was brief. Kitty did not find the area to be as exciting as she had heard it had been during the gold rush. To earn the thousands she hoped as an entertainer and gambler, she needed to be in a place where new gold was being pulled out of the streams and hills. California's findings were old and nearly played out. Kitty boarded a stage alone and headed for a new gold boomtown in the Black Hills of South Dakota.

Deadwood Gulch, South Dakota, was teeming with more than six thousand eager prospectors, most of whom spent their hard earnings at the faro tables in saloons. Kitty hired on at the notorious Gem Theatre and danced her way to the same popularity she had experienced in Dallas. Enamored miners competed for her attention, but none seemed to hold her interest. It wasn't until she met Sam Curley that the thought of spending an extended period of time with one man seemed appealing.

Thirty-five-year-old Sam was a cardsharp with a reputation as a peaceful man who felt more at home behind a poker table than anywhere else. Kitty and Sam had a lot in common, and their mutual attraction blossomed into a proposal of marriage. On June 10, 1877, the pair exchanged vows at the Gem Theatre on the same stage where Kitty performed. Unbeknownst to the cheering onlookers and the groom, however, Kitty was already married. Her first husband lived in Bay City, Michigan, with her son, who had been born in 1872. Bored with the trappings of a traditional home life, Kitty had abandoned the pair to travel the West.

When Sam learned that he was married to a bigamist, he was upset, and the pair quarreled. He was not only dissatisfied with his marital status,

Wearing a come-hither look and inviting smile, lovely lady gamblers enticed trail-blazers and cowhands to frequent saloons.

but also fiercely unhappy with the law enforcement in the rough town. He didn't like Sheriff Seth Bullock's "strong arm tactics," and within six months of marrying Kitty, he left Deadwood Gulch for Colorado.

Perhaps she was distraught over the abrupt departure of her current husband, but Kitty's congenial personality suddenly turned cold and unfriendly. She was distrusting of patrons and began carrying six-shooters in her skirt pockets and a Bowie knife in the folds of the deep curls of her hair. She moved from Deadwood Gulch to Central City, where she ran a saloon. Because she was always heavily armed, she was able to keep the wild residents who frequented her establishment under control.

Restless and unable to get beyond Sam's absence, Kitty returned to Deadwood and opened a combination brothel and gambling parlor. She called her place the Mint and enticed many miners to her faro table, where she quickly relieved them of their gold dust. On one particularly profitable evening, she raked in more than $8,000. A braggadocious German industrialist had challenged her to a game and lost. The debate continues among historians as to whether Kitty cheated her way to the expensive win. Most believe she was a less than honest dealer.

Kitty's profession and seductive manner of dress sparked rumors that she had had many lovers and had been married five times. Kitty never denied the rumors and even added to them by boasting that she had been courted by hundreds of eligible bachelors and "lost track of the number of times men had proposed" to her. Because she carried a variety of weapons on her at all times, rumors also abounded that she had shot or stabbed more than a dozen gamblers for cheating at cards. She never denied those tales, either.

By the fall of 1877, the torch Kitty carried for Sam was temporarily extinguished by a former lover. The two spent many nights at the Lone Star Saloon and eventually moved in together.

News of Kitty's romantic involvement reached a miserable Sam, who had established a faro game at a posh saloon in Cheyenne, Wyoming. Sam was furious about being replaced and immediately purchased a ticket back to Deadwood. Hoping to catch Kitty alone with her lover, he disguised his looks and changed his name.

When Sam arrived in town on December 6, 1877, he couldn't bring himself to face the pair in person. He sent a message to Kitty's paramour to meet with him instead, but the man refused. In a fit of rage Sam told one of the Lone Star Saloon employees that he intended to kill his unfaithful wife and then himself.

Frustrated and desperate, Sam sent a note to Kitty, pleading with her to meet him at the Lone Star Saloon. She reluctantly agreed. Not long after Kitty ascended the stairs of the tavern, patrons heard her scream followed by the sound of two gunshots.

A reporter for the *Black Hills Daily Times* visited the scene of the murder-suicide the morning after the event occurred. "The bodies were dressed and lying side by side in the room of death," he later wrote in an article for the newspaper. "Suspended upon the wall, a pretty picture of Kitty, taken when the bloom and vigor of youth gazed down upon the tenements of clay, as if to enable the visitor to contrast a happy past with a most wretched present. The pool of blood rested upon the floor; blood stains were upon the door and walls. . . . The cause of the tragedy may be summed up in a few words; aye, in one 'jealousy.'"

A simple funeral was held for the pair at the same location where they had met their end. Although they were placed in separate pine caskets, they were buried in the same grave at the Ingleside Cemetery. According to the January 7, 1878, edition of the *Black Hills Daily Times*, Kitty had "drawn a holographic will in ink on the day prior to her death." Her estate amounted to $650. A portion of the funds was used to pay for the service, burial, and tombstone.

It seems that Kitty LeRoy and Sam Curley's spirits would not rest after they were lowered into their shared grave. A month after the pair had departed from this world, their ghosts were reportedly haunting the Lone Star Saloon. Patrons claim the phantoms appeared to "recline in loving embraces and finally melt away in the shadows of the night."

The editor of the *Black Hills Daily Times* pursued the story of the "disembodied spirits" and, after investigating the disturbances, wrote an article on the subject that was printed on February 28, 1878.

The Lone Star building gained its first notoriety from the suicide, by poisoning, of a woman of ill repute last spring. The house was subsequently rented by Hattie Donnelly, and for a time all went smoothly,

*with the exception of such little sounds and disturbances as are inci-
dent to such places. About the first of December the house was rented
by Kitty LeRoy, a woman said to be well connected and possessed of
intelligence far beyond her class. Kitty was a woman well known to
the reporter, and whatever might have been her life here, it is not
necessary to display her virtues or her vices, as we deal simply with
information gleaned from hearsay and observation. With the above
facts before the reader we simply give the following, as it appeared to
us, and leave the readers to draw their own conclusions as to the phe-
nomena witnessed by ourselves and many others. It is an oft repeated
tale, but one which in this case is lent more than ordinary interest by
the tragic events surrounding the actors.*

*To tell our tale briefly and simply, is to repeat a story old and well
known—the reappearance, in spirit form, of departed humanity. In this
case it is the shadow of a woman, comely, if not beautiful, and always following her footsteps, the tread and form of the man who was the cause of
their double death. In the still watches of the night, the double phantoms
are seen to tread the stairs where once they reclined in the flesh and linger
o'er places where once they reclined in loving embrace, and finally to melt
away in the shadows of the night as peacefully as their bodies' souls seem
to have done when the fatal bullets brought death and the grave to each.*

*Whatever may have been the vices and virtues of the ill-starred
and ill-mated couple, we trust their spirits may find a happier camp-
ing ground than the hills and gulches of the Black Hills, and that tho'
infelicity reign with them here happiness may blossom in a fairer
climate.*

The bodies of Kitty LeRoy and Sam Curley were eventually moved
to the mountaintop cemetery of Mount Moriah in Deadwood and their
burial spots left unidentified.

Tessie Wall

Barbary Coast Madam

"Drink that up, boys! Have a drink on Tessie Wall!"
MADAM TESSIE WALL'S INVITATION TO OFFICERS
AT THE ANNUAL POLICEMAN'S BALL AFTER
LAYING A $1,000 BILL ON THE BAR, 1913

A parade of horse-drawn carriages deposited fashionably dressed San Francisco citizens at the entrance of the Tivoli Theatre. A handsome couple, holding hands and cooing as young lovers do, emerged from one of the vehicles. A figure across the street, hidden in the shadows of an alleyway, eyed the pair intently. Once the couple entered the building, Tessie Wall stepped out of the darkness into the subdued light of a row of gas lamps lining the busy thoroughfare. Tears streamed down the svelte blonde's face. The pain of seeing the man she loved with another woman was unbearable.

Several hours before, Tessie and her ex-husband, Frank Daroux, had entertained passersby with a robust argument over the other woman in his life. After accusing the man of being a liar and a thief, Tessie begged him for another chance and promised to make him forget anyone else with whom he was involved. Frank angrily warned Tessie that if she started anything he would put her "so far away that no one would find her."

The words he had said to her played over and over again in her head. "You've got my husband," she mumbled to herself. "And you'll get yours someday. It's not right." She choked back a torrent of tears, reached into her handbag, and removed a silver-plated revolver. Hiding the weapon in the folds of her dress, she stepped back into the dark alleyway and waited.

It wasn't long until Frank walked out of the theater, alone. Standing on the steps of the building, he lit up a cigar and cast a glance into the night sky. Preoccupied with his view of the stars, Frank did not see Tessie

A view inside Madam Tessie Wall's elaborate house of ill fame in San Francisco
SAN FRANCISCO HISTORY CENTER, SAN FRANCISCO PUBLIC LIBRARY

hurry across the street and race over to him. Before he realized what was happening, Tessie pointed the gun at his chest and fired. As Frank fell backward he grabbed hold of the rim of a nearby carriage Tessie unloaded two more shots into his upper body. Frank collapsed in a bloody heap.

Tessie stood over his near-lifeless frame, sobbing. When the police arrived she was kneeling beside Frank, the gun still clutched in her hand. When asked why she opened fire on him, she wailed, "I shot him 'cause I love him, Goddamn him!"

Tessie Wall was one of the Barbary Coast's most popular madams. Since entering the business in 1898, her life had been mired in controversy. Born on May 26, 1869, she was one of ten children. Her mother, who died at the age of forty-four, named her chubby, ash-blond daughter Teresa Susan Donahue. Her father, Eugene, was a dock worker and spent a considerable amount of time away from home. Teresa and her brothers and sisters took care of themselves. By the time she turned thirteen, Teresa, or Tessie as she was referred to by friends and family, had developed into a beautiful, curvaceous young woman. She turned heads everywhere she went in the Mission District, where she lived.

In 1884 Tessie accepted a marriage proposal from Edward M. Wall, a handsome fireman twice her age. Edward was a heavy drinker and was often out of work because of his "weakness." Tessie supported them with her job as a housekeeper. Two years after the pair married they had a son. Joseph Lawrence Wall's life was short. He died four months after his birth from respiratory complications. Tessie was devastated and, following her husband's example, took up drinking to dull the pain.

Joseph's death had an adverse effect on Edward and Tessie's relationship. Both blamed the other for their loss. The Walls' marriage ended in bitter divorce. Historians believe heartbreak over her child's death and the subsequent demise of her marriage contributed to Tessie's decision to enter into a life of prostitution.

Before venturing out on her own, Tessie continued to keep house for some of San Francisco's most prominent citizens. While in their employ Tessie learned about the unconventional desires and habits many of the elite society members possessed. After learning how much money they were willing to pay for their debauchery, she decided to go into business for herself. In 1898 she purchased a brothel and hired a stable of beautiful young ladies to work for her.

In two years Tessie's "lodging house" had become so successful that she was able to open a second brothel.

Tessie's bordellos were visited by some of the wealthiest businessmen and politicians in the state. Upon entering, her business clients were greeted by elegantly dressed women offering them wine and champagne. The home itself was equally inviting and posh. It was furnished with antiques, plush red-velvet sofas and armchairs, and a large gold fireplace. The draperies and bedroom furniture were just as ornate. Tessie had a giant, gold Napoleon bed decorated with swans and cupids. The dresser and matching mirror were gilded in gold.

Madam Wall's parlor house was recognized as one of the best in the city. Tessie herself would spend time with her guests before they left with a lady of their choosing. She listened intently to their stories about life and work and would laugh uproariously at their jokes. Patrons were so captivated by the charms of their host that they often admitted that when they sat down in the parlor and started talking to Tessie, they forgot what they came for.

Tessie knew the importance of advertising. The method she used to promote her house was unconventional but effective. She would clothe her girls in the latest garments from Paris and New York and send them out on the street for all to admire. Every Saturday afternoon, Tessie's girls would hold a parade on Market Street. Everyone in the neighborhood would come out to see the new fashions being worn by the demimonde.

Once other madams saw how popular the parades were, they launched their own exhibitions. It wasn't uncommon on weekends to see numerous women marching on opposite sides of the thoroughfare, modeling the latest styles. Parlor houses with the best showing reaped the benefits in the evening. Due in large part to Tessie's welcoming personality and the voluptuous ladies that worked for her, Tessie's brothel was usually the one that did the most business.

Madam Wall's parlor house yielded a sizeable profit, but the opportunities the income afforded her and the conversation she enjoyed with an array of customers couldn't keep her from thinking about her son. During those melancholy moments she would once again turn to alcohol. By this point in her life, Tessie was able to consume enormous quantities of wine and drink most men under the table. Often she challenged beer drinkers to champagne drinking contests. The famous boxer John L. Sullivan was one such participant. Sullivan was unaccustomed to the effects of champagne, and after twenty-one drinks he passed out. Still standing after twenty-two drinks, Tessie won the contest and was forever referred to as "the woman who licked John L. Sullivan."

The life and business Madam Wall had built was almost destroyed by the great fire of 1906. A massive earthquake rocked San Francisco on August 1, causing electric lights to fall, spark, and set fire to buildings and homes along Market Street. The blaze spread throughout the city, reducing multiple structures to ash.

Despite her best efforts, Tessie's parlor house did not survive the inferno. The only item she managed to save was the gold fireplace. When she rebuilt the brothel a year later, the resilient item was put back in place. It became the focal point of the house and the subject of much conversation for years to come.

The new parlor house was just as popular as before, but competition from new rival houses had heightened. Jessie Hayman, the madam from a high-class establishment near Tessie's, had attracted many clients, and her business continued to grow daily. Madam Wall was forced to come up with fresh ways to promote her house.

In addition to the weekly parades of her employees dressed in their finest, Tessie decided to show off her staff at music halls and theaters. Every Sunday evening Tessie and her ladies would attend a vaudeville performance at the Orpheum Theatre. She purposely arrived late so all eyes would be focused on her beauties as they made their way to their seats.

The stunt drastically increased nightly business. When Jessie learned what Tessie was doing, she began taking her ladies to the theater, too. On Sunday nights the two madams would try to best each other with grand entrances that seemed to upstage the performers. Determined not to be outdone, Tessie decided to keep her girls from attending a couple of shows. The spectacle of their arrival always generated a lot of attention, and she hoped their absence would do the same.

The empty seats did pique the public's interest, and just as the conversation about where they were died down, Tessie and her ladies returned. As the lights dimmed, the curtain went up, the music started, and Madam Wall and her girls made their way down the aisle. As though on cue, the show suddenly stopped, the house lights were turned up again, and all eyes were on Tessie and her ladies.

For every public attempt to increase business there were private deals being made to do the same. It was not uncommon for hotel clerks, bellboys, headwaiters, chefs at restaurants, and cabbies to be paid handsome sums to direct wealthy men to the finer parlor houses. Such help was generally worth 10 percent of the amount earned from that customer.

Over her long career Tessie made friends with several well-known figures. One such man was politician Milton Latham, who would later become the governor of California. At the time of their meeting, he was a struggling architect. Tessie was struggling herself. A public outcry against houses like hers from moral citizens prompted city officials to place restrictions on a madam's ability to add more rooms to her business. Construction on a new house of ill repute was also restricted.

In spite of the limitations, Latham wanted to build Tessie a new bordello. Madam Wall laughed at the thought and reminded him of the police blockade on houses like hers. "It's so strict right now," she told Latham, "that I can't even put out red lights or hang red shades." After Latham managed to convince Tessie that it was doable and his offer was sincere, she agreed to try to acquire a building permit. To her surprise, she was granted one.

Latham built an exquisite home in the city's Tenderloin district. The three-story terra-cotta structure had twelve suites, a large kitchen and dining room, a saloon, three parlors, and a ballroom. An average of fourteen women lived and worked at the house. Some came to the ornate business from as far away as France. The majority of Madam Wall's highly sought-after employees were young and blond. A thirty-something brunette known as Black Gladys garnered the most attention at the home.

Madam Wall's parlor house at 337 O'Farrell Street was a popular stop for college men and young entrepreneurs. Tessie's clients could pay for the services of her ladies by cash or credit and did not normally spend the night. If gentlemen did stay overnight, however, they were sent on their way only after their clothes were pressed, and they were served a full breakfast.

Among the many repeat customers at Tessie's establishment was Frank Daroux. Frank was a gambler and politician. He held a high-ranking position within the Republican Party and had a weakness for brothels. One evening in 1909, he wandered into Tessie's place and was instantly captivated by the flamboyant madam. She was equally charmed by him. Frank invited Tessie to dinner, and the two laughed and conversed through an elaborate meal.

The evening left a lasting impression on Frank, not merely because the company was stimulating but because Tessie drank a considerable amount of wine. In addition to the fine French food the pair was served in a private dining room, Tessie enjoyed twenty glasses of champagne and never left the table.

Tessie was attracted to Frank for a variety of reasons. He resembled Napoleon—a man she thought was devilishly handsome. And he was clever, smart, and well respected in the community. It was that kind of respectability for which Tessie longed. After a whirlwind courtship and significant persuasion on her part, the pair was married.

Frank felt his career in politics would suffer if it was widely known he married a madam, so he insisted the wedding take place out of town and then be kept a secret. Tessie reluctantly agreed to his terms but made him promise she could host a party to celebrate their commitment to one another. One hundred guests attended the grand affair. They were treated to a delicious feast and eighty cases of champagne.

The Darouxes' marriage was rocky from the start. Preoccupied with his public image, Frank demanded Tessie remove herself as madam and run the business in a more covert manner. Tessie agreed, hoping the action would also allow the two to spend more time together. Frank, however, often left his new wife alone while he oversaw the activities at various gambling houses he owned. When he was home neighbors would overhear the pair loudly arguing in the early hours of the morning.

The difficulties between the two worsened when a new mayor and city council, bent on reform, were elected to office. The conservative public servants wanted to stamp out gambling and prostitution in San Francisco. Once the Darouxes' livelihoods were threatened, they turned on one another.

In an effort to convince politicians that his business practices and personal life were respectable, Frank removed himself even further from his bride. He befriended the new elected officials, convincing them that profits earned from his establishment could financially benefit them and the city. He attended posh social engagements and rallies unaccompanied by Madam Wall.

The more politically powerful Frank became, the more he tried to persuade Tessie to sell the parlor house. He reasoned that if she got out of the business it would ultimately make him look better once news of their marriage became common knowledge. As further enticement to give up the parlor house, Frank purchased a home for Tessie in the country. The gesture did not bring about the desired result. Tessie refused to leave the bustle of the city. "I'd rather be an electric light pole on Powell Street," she told her husband, "than own all the land in the sticks."

No matter how much she might have questioned the wisdom of marrying a man who did not accept her as she was, Tessie's dreams of being embraced socially by San Francisco's elite never wavered. She longed to be invited to chic affairs where important and well-respected guests appeared.

By the spring of 1911, she had managed to acquire an invitation to the Greenway Cotillion, a dinner and dance held to honor the city's founding fathers. The invitation, for Madam Wall and twelve of her girls, was procured by a politician and regular guest of the parlor house and came with a stipulation. If the ladies chose to attend, their identities had to be disguised by champagne bottle costumes they would be required to wear. Tessie agreed.

Her appearance at the cotillion, even if it was disguised, impelled an unnamed socialite to invite Madam Wall to the annual Mardi Gras ball. Wearing tails and a top hat, Frank attended the gala with his wife. Tessie's dress was tasteful and understated. She was disappointed but not surprised that her name was not listed in the local newspaper as one of the Mardi Gras attendees. She remedied the omission by reporting the loss of an expensive diamond broach at the location of the ball. The report was followed by a lost and found article placed in the *San Francisco Examiner*. Everyone who read the newspaper that day knew the notorious O'Farrell Street madam had been at the Mardi Gras ball.

Having managed to get herself on the guest list for many more engagements, Tessie was able to convince Frank that she was no longer political poison and was now worthy of a church wedding. Frank consented to a public ceremony but was adamant about Tessie retiring from the business.

This time she acquiesced and transferred the management of the house to one of her employees. Given the magnitude of the sacrifice, Tessie expected Frank to do something for her. At her request he promised to make all the arrangements for the reception and agreed to her guest list, choice of music, and location.

Once a priest who would marry them was secured, a wedding date was set. Nearly two years from the date Frank and Tessie were initially married, the two renewed their vows. The second ceremony was held in the rectory of St. Mary's Cathedral on July 11, 1911.

Within hours of the nuptials, the Darouxes were exchanging insults. Frank had disregarded all of Tessie's requests for the reception, and she verbalized her irritation in a toast where she announced that she was returning to her parlor house business as quickly as she could. Toward the end of the evening, the pair had once again reconciled. Frank took that opportunity of brief calm to present his wife with a wedding gift. News of the expensive gesture of affection was published in the *San Francisco Chronicle* the following day, with the headline "$10,000 Pearl Necklace Wedding Gift to Bride/Frank Daroux Marries Miss Theresa Donahue."

After a brief honeymoon Frank and Tessie returned to the lives they had made for themselves. Frank kept active in politics and oversaw business at his gambling dens. Tessie focused on her brothel. Religious groups staunchly opposed to parlor houses began a crusade to drive them out of business. Madam Wall's place was a prime target. Frank did nothing to stop the powers that be from threatening her livelihood. But that was the least of her problems. Unbeknownst to Tessie, her husband was betraying her in a more profound way.

The Darouxes' relationship had always been a volatile one. They never shied away from quarreling in public. Frank grew tired of the embarrassing outbursts and was frustrated with the way it was diminishing his influence on key political figures. His attention eventually turned to a less combative woman he met at a fundraiser. In 1915 the two began having an affair. Tessie found the pair and vowed to kill the woman if she came near her husband again. Frank stayed in the marriage another two years before walking out on Tessie and filing for divorce.

Like all of the other disagreements Tessie and Frank had in their eight years of marriage, the fight over how their union would end was made public as well.

Tessie made it clear to all who would listen that she did not want to lose Frank, and she contested the divorce numerous times. After a long and vicious court battle, the marriage was finally dissolved.

Tessie returned to her house to nurse her wounds. Her heart was broken. She couldn't accept that Frank was officially out of her life. In a desperate attempt to win him back, she secretly followed him around, waiting for a chance to speak with him and convince him to return to her.

The evening Frank was shot, the two had quarreled over Tessie's threat to appeal the divorce. Frank warned his ex-wife that he'd "break her" if she went through with the action. He hurled a string of obscenities at her as he turned and walked away. She heard from a friend that Frank and his mistress were going to attend the theater that evening, and she decided to confront the two there.

"Then I didn't know what I did," Tessie explained to the police after the shooting. When asked about the gun, Tessie told authorities that she bought it because of the other woman. "That woman took my husband away from me," she cried. "For three or four years she has been going with him. It made me mad." Tessie pleaded with police to take her to the hospital where Frank was so she could see him.

As they transported the sobbing madam to the sanitarium, she professed her undying love for her "darling husband."

Frank was conscious when Tessie entered the emergency room. The three bullets she had emptied into his upper torso had missed his vital organs. Doctors expected him to make a full recovery. The police escorted Tessie to his bedside and asked Frank if she was the one who shot him. "Yes, she shot me," he responded. "Take her away. I don't want to see her." According to the *San Francisco Chronicle*, "Tessie Daroux lifted her handkerchief to her face in a gesture of horror and reeled back into the arms of the officer."

Madam Wall was booked on a charge of intent to kill and held without bail for three months. Bail was finally granted when Frank was given a clean bill of health. In a move that surprised everyone, Frank announced to authorities that he had made a decision not to press charges against Tessie. She took the news as a sign of his continued affection for her and filed an appeal on the divorce. Frank had hoped the incident and his willingness not to prosecute would drive Tessie away. Once he found out that she was appealing the divorce, he changed his mind about pressing charges.

The shooting and subsequent court activity were front page news. The scandal wreaked havoc on Frank's political future. His peers informed him that he was a liability and suggested relocating. Frank agreed and reversed his decision again about having Tessie prosecuted and made arrangements to marry his mistress.

Days before Frank was to marry the other woman, Madam Wall again took gun in hand. This time she set out to kill her rival. When she found her eating lunch at a popular restaurant, Tessie shot through the glass window at the future Mrs. Daroux. Her aim was poor, and the woman was not hit. Tessie was arrested, and, while she was being held, Frank remarried. With the stipulation that Tessie not be released until they left town, Mr. and Mrs. Daroux agreed not to press charges. Frank and his bride then moved to the East Coast.

Madam Wall went back to her parlor house, boxed up all of the busts and paintings she had of Napoleon, and stored them away. She never fully retired from the trade and remained a controversial figure throughout the duration of her life.

On the morning of April 28, 1932, Tessie pulled an impacted tooth that had been bothering her. That evening she died of a hemorrhage following the extraction.

Newspapers marked her passing with an obituary Tessie had preapproved.

"One more bit of 'the San Francisco that was' has drifted off in that uncharted Sargasso that holds the old Barbary Coast, the Poodle Dog, the Silver Dollar, the Bank Exchange, the Mason Street Tenderloin and those other gay haunts that made San Francisco famous through the Seven Seas," proclaimed the *San Francisco Chronicle* on April 30, 1932.

Mrs. Teresa Susan Wall Daroux was sixty-two years old.

Lottie Deno

The Cosmopolitan Gambler

"She subdues the reckless, subjugates the religious, sobers the frivolous, burns the ground from under the indolent moccasins of that male she's roped up in holy wedlock's bonds, and points the way to a higher, happier life."

AUTHOR ALFRED HENRY LEWIS'S
DESCRIPTION OF LOTTIE DENO, 1913

A broad grin spread across Doc Holliday's thin, unshaven face as he tossed five playing cards facedown into the center of a rustic, wooden table. His eyes followed a petite, gloved hand as it swept a pile of poker chips toward a demure, dark-haired beauty sitting opposite him. Lottie Deno watched the infamous dentist, gambler, and gunfighter lean back in his chair and pour himself a shot of whiskey. Doc's steely blue eyes met hers and she held his gaze. "You want to lose any more of your money to me or is that it, Doc?" "Deal," he responded confidently. Lottie did as he asked and in a few short minutes had managed to win another hand.

A crowd of customers at the Bee Hive Saloon in Fort Griffin, Texas, slowly made their way over to the table where Lottie and Doc had squared off. They cheered the cardsharps on and bought them drinks. Most of the time Lottie won the hands. The talented poker players continued on until dawn. When the chips were added up, the lady gambler had acquired more than $30,000 of Holliday's money.

"If one must gamble they should settle on three things at the start," Doc said before drinking down another shot. "And they are?" Lottie inquired. "Decide the rules of the game, the stakes, and the quitting time." Holliday smoothed down his shirt and coat, adjusted his hat, and nodded politely to the onlookers. "Good evening to you all," he said as he made his way to the exit. Lottie smiled to herself as she sorted her chips. Holliday sauntered out of the saloon and into the bright morning light.

Historians maintain that it was only natural that Lottie Deno would have grown up to be an expert poker player—her father was a part-time gambler who had taught his daughter everything he knew about cards. She is recognized by many gaming historians as the most talented woman to play five-card draw in the West.

Lottie was born Carlotta J. Thompkins in Warsaw, Kentucky, on April 21, 1844. She was the eldest of the two girls her parents would have. Her mother and father had amassed a substantial amount of money tobacco farming. They lavished their children with every advantage possible, including travel. Her father took his oldest child with him on business trips to New Orleans and Detroit. At both locations he escorted his daughter to the finest gambling houses and introduced her to the art of poker, roulette, horse racing, and faro. Lottie's seven-foot-tall nanny, Mary Poindexter, accompanied the pair on every journey. By the time Lottie was sixteen, she was a skilled card player often in need of protection from gamblers she fleeced. Mary made sure her charge never got hurt.

The attack on South Carolina's Fort Sumter in April 1861 outraged many Southerners, prompting them to enlist in the Confederate Army. Lottie's father was no exception. Six hundred and eighteen thousand men lost their lives over the course of the Civil War. Lottie's father was killed in the first engagement he fought.

The news of Thompkins's death devastated his daughters and wife. Lottie's mother's health immediately began to fail.

The now seventeen-year-old girl assumed the role of head of the family and took over the business of the Thompkins plantation. Distant family members, who felt it was inappropriate for a female to be in such a position, persuaded Lottie's mother to send her away. She agreed and Lottie was sent to Detroit to live with friends. Her mother hoped she would meet a suitable man to marry there.

Lottie arrived in the city at the peak of the social season, and the limited funds her mother supplied her with did not last long. Expenses had been much more than anticipated. Back home in Kentucky, Lottie's mother and sister were struggling financially as well. The war had left the plantation in disarray, and the lack of workers prevented the crops from being planted. When news of the hardship her family was enduring reached Lottie, she decided to get a job.

An invitation to visit a gambling fraternity provided a way for her to earn an income. Lottie's talent for winning at the poker tables gave her enough money to send home and support herself in style. No questions were asked as to how Lottie came into the money and no explanation was offered.

Lottie not only jeopardized her social standing in the community by frequenting the gambling house, but also exposed herself to a cast of unsavory characters. It was there she made the acquaintance of a charming but ruthless gambler named Johnny Golden. Golden was from Boston and was of Jewish descent. Lottie's mother and other family members, as well as a large percentage of the population at the time, were anti-Semitic. Lottie was strongly chastised for her association with Golden, but that only made him more endearing to her.

The couple gambled together and lived together unmarried for a time. Johnny was not as lucky in cards as Lottie. His misfortune at the poker table, combined with the difficulties he experienced as a Jew, led to the two parting company. Golden headed back east and Lottie moved on to Louisiana.

News of her mother's death reached Lottie just as she was settling into a hotel in New Orleans. She was brokenhearted and lonesome for her sister. She wanted to make sure her sister was generously cared for and given the opportunity to continue her education. In an effort to make that happen, Lottie found steady poker games on the riverboats that traveled the waterways through the southeast. She made a lot of money, enough to put her sister through private school. Once the sister graduated, Lottie purchased a train ticket for her sibling to meet her in San Antonio, Texas.

Lottie was restless and bored with New Orleans when she set out for Texas in May 1865. San Antonio was an exciting city, teaming with new gambling parlors and betting houses. Games of chance weren't restricted to evening entertainment, either. The opportunity to make a fortune was open to professional gamblers and gaming enthusiasts twenty-four hours a day.

Wearing fashionable garments of lace and tulle and batting their long lashes at unsuspecting gamblers, women enticed men to roulette and dice tables. Whether the men won or lost, the women received a share of the bets placed on the games from the gambling den.
THE DENVER PUBLIC LIBRARY, WESTERN HISTORY COLLECTION, X-2946

Lottie played poker at the Cosmopolitan Club, a posh saloon and casino near Alamo Plaza. After seeing her play, the owner of a rival business known as the University Club offered her a job as house gambler at his establishment. A house gambler used money the saloon provided to play poker. The professional card player would invite patrons to join in a few hands with the express purpose of separating them from their cash or property. The house gambler received a percentage of the winnings.

Lottie's beauty and the novelty of seeing a woman gambler attracted a lot of men to the saloon. She waited at the poker table like a spider waiting for her victims to wander into her web. Many University Club patrons referred to Lottie as the "Angel of San Antonio."

Dressed in the finest styles available in New Orleans, dealing cards and batting her large, dark eyes at customers, she was a popular inducement. Besides five-card draw, her specialty was a game called faro. The game, which originated in France, was one of the most popular in the West.

Frank Thurmond, the owner of the University Club, had more than a professional interest in Lottie. Not long after she began working at the saloon, the two became romantically involved. Their love affair was short lived, however. Thurmond was forced to leave town after stabbing a disorderly patron and killing him. Lottie left the area soon afterward to find him. It was rumored that Frank had headed west. Lottie did the same. She arrived in Fort Concho, Texas, in early 1870 needing additional travel money to go on. She quickly found a game at a local saloon and in no time was impressing cowhands and drifters who sat across from her at a poker or faro table.

Lottie refused to say what had brought her from San Antonio to Fort Concho. She was afraid she might cause trouble for Frank if she admitted publicly that she was looking for him. It was the evasiveness about where she came from and where she was headed that prompted people to start calling her Mystic Maude.

From Fort Concho she traveled to Jacksboro, San Angelo, Denison, and Fort Worth. At each stop she gambled, winning hand after hand. When one town was played out, she moved on to another. Her actions led many to speculate that she was waiting for a man to meet her. Some guessed he might be an outlaw. Lottie avoided conversation on the subject and redirected the curious back to the cards she dealt them.

A few humiliated gamblers who had the misfortune of losing to Lottie believed she was a cheat. "The likelihood of a woman being able to win enough pots to make a living playing cards is farfetched," a saloonkeeper in El Paso told a newspaper reporter in 1872. "That could only happen if she were crooked."

If Lottie was dishonest at cards, she was as good at not being detected as she was at the game. Most onlookers focused on her winnings rather than her actual game. The fortune she amassed in one night at the tables in Fort Griffin, Texas, brought her a lot of attention and a new name.

She had won several hands in a row and was stacking her chips in a neat pile when a drunk ranch hand standing nearby yelled out, "Honey, with winnings like them, you ought to call yourself Lotta Dinero."

Of all the handles she had acquired in her career, it was the name she thought suited her best. She shortened the nom de plume to Lottie Deno and used it the rest of her life.

Fort Griffin had a reputation for being one of the roughest towns in the West. Outside of a few shady ladies, the burg was populated primarily by young, rowdy men, former Confederate soldiers distressed about the way the Civil War had ended. It was a volatile environment where Lottie thrived and had great success as a gambler.

Lottie hosted a regular game at the Bee Hive Saloon in Fort Griffin and was treated like royalty by the men who frequented the business. Bartender Mike Fogarty treated her especially well. Fogarty, it would later be determined, was in fact Frank Thurmond. Still fearful of being found out by the law, Thurmond and Lottie would steal away to a nearby town for secret rendezvous. The couple's true relationship remained hidden from the public until they were married in December 1880.

In addition to seeing thousands of dollars come and go, Lottie witnessed her share of violence at the tables. Most of the time she watched disinterested at the explosive action of the drunken miner or cowboy who lost numerous poker hands. The atmosphere of a smoky saloon, the endless supply of alcohol, and distractions from sporting girls helped create the occasional sore loser.

One evening when Lottie was dealing faro, an argument involving a pair of fledgling gamblers broke out at a table adjacent to her. The fight became physical and shots were then exchanged. Fort Griffin sheriff Bill

Cruger intervened, killing both men who drew on him as he hurried into the saloon to settle things. With the exception of Lottie, everyone in the saloon had fled when the bullets started flying.

Sheriff Cruger was amazed at Lottie's demeanor and commented to her that he couldn't understand why she had stayed at the scene. "You've never been a desperate woman, Sheriff," she calmly told him. Lottie was immune to such tensions. Her focus was on winning the pot. Enduring the temper of unfortunate card players went with the territory. She never feared for her life, but she did fear being poor.

Lottie's monetary drive, beauty, and talent captured the attention of many colorful frontier characters. Authors, songwriters, and artists painted pictures of the lady gambler and penned stories about her vivacious, unconventional spirit.

Dan Quin, a cowhand turned writer, wrote a series of books about his adventures through the Old West, and one story featured a gambler fitting the description of Lottie Deno. In the book Quin, who used the pen name Alfred Henry Lewis, renamed Lottie "Faro Nell."

Faro Nell was "a handsome lady with a steady hand and quick mind made for flipping the pasteboards." Lewis's book, published in 1913, helped immortalize the lady gambler. However, Lottie was not flattered by the publication. She saw it as an "unfair representation" showing her as an "unsophisticated lady without proper breeding."

After dealing various games at the Bee Hive Saloon for five years, Lottie left Fort Griffin and headed to Kingston, New Mexico, where she again met up with Frank. The pair went into business together in mid-1878. They established a gambling room at the Victorio Hotel in Kingston and opened a saloon in nearby Silver City. Both towns were booming from the gold and silver strikes in the area, and miners were eager to part with a few dollars by drinking and playing cards.

Lottie and Frank not only were making money hand over fist, but also had acquired several mining claims that had been put up as bets. The pair became so wealthy that they began lending money to mining operations in exchange for a stake in their findings. The couple used a portion of their income to get married and establish a home. They exchanged vows on December 2, 1880, at the Silver City courthouse.

Lottie continued working, by night dealing cards and by day managing the Thurmonds' two saloons, restaurant, and a hotel they now owned. She also ventured into charity work, providing room and board for newly released prisoners.

In 1883 Lottie and her husband purchased a liquor distribution business in Deming, New Mexico, another growing gold mining town. They also bought property in the heart of town and a large ranch at the base of the mountains surrounding the ever-developing city.

If not for the brutal murder of a gambler by the name of Dan Baxter, Lottie might have stayed on as a house faro dealer at the saloon she and Frank owned in Silver City. Little is known of the actual event. It started with a quarrel between Baxter and Frank. Baxter threw a billiard ball at Frank, and Frank pulled out a knife and stabbed him in the abdomen. Baxter died. Law enforcement determined that Frank acted in self-defense, but the incident forced Lottie to reevaluate her career choice. She was tired of the senseless violence that accompanied her line of work and decided to retire.

Lottie and Frank settled down in Deming to live a quiet, orderly existence. Frank focused his attention on the mines, land, and cattle ranches they jointly owned. Lottie became involved with civic organizations and helped build an Episcopal church.

The second half of Lottie's life was tame compared to the first half. She adapted easily to the role of proper wife and respected community leader, trading in a hand of poker for a game of bridge and helping to form a local association called the Golden Gossip Club. The social club, which still exists today, was made up primarily of wives of leading businessmen. They got together to quilt, swap recipes, and play cards.

In 1908, after having been with Lottie for more than forty years, Frank died of cancer. Lottie lived another twenty-six years after her husband's death. On February 9, 1934, at the age of eighty-nine, she became critically ill and died. The local daily newspaper, the *Deming Graphic*, noted that she "maintained her usual cheerful spirit to the last."

The memory of Lottie Deno has been kept alive in feature films and television programs. Motion picture historians maintain that the characters Laura Denbow in the movie *Gunfight at the O.K. Corral* and Miss Kitty in the television show *Gunsmoke* are based on Lottie Deno.

Julia Bulette

Siren of the Silver Town

"Every city in the civilized world must have its soiled doves. It is a necessary evil."

BAKERSFIELD *CALIFORNIAN*, OCTOBER 25, 1892

The cold, gray January sky above Virginia City, Nevada, in 1867 unleashed a torrent of sleet on a slow-moving funeral procession traveling along the main thoroughfare of town. Several members of the volunteer fire department, Virginia Engine Company Number One, were first in a long line of mourners following a horse-drawn carriage transporting the body of soiled dove Julia Bulette. The Nevada militia band shuffled behind the hearse playing "The Girl I Left Behind Me." Black wreaths and streamers hung from the balconies of the buildings lining the route along which the remains of the beloved thirty-five-year-old woman were escorted. Miners who knew Julia wept openly. Out of respect for the deceased woman, all the saloons were closed. Plummeting temperatures and icy winds eventually drove the majority of funeral-goers inside their homes and businesses before Julia was lowered into the ground.

Julia was murdered on January 19, 1867, at eleven thirty in the evening in her home on North D Street in Virginia City. The fair but frail prostitute told her neighbor and best friend Gertrude Holmes she was expecting company, but did not specify who the company might be. Twelve hours later Gertrude discovered Julia's lifeless body in bed. She had been beaten and strangled. Gertrude told authorities that Julia was lying in the center of the bed with the blankets pulled over her head and that the sheets under her frame were smooth. She told police that it appeared as though no one had ever been in the bed with Julia.

The authorities believed the scene had been staged. Marks on Julia's body and tears on the pillow used to smother her indicated she struggled with her attacker. The murderer then set the room to look as though nothing was out of the ordinary. He covered Julia's body in such a way that at a passing glance she would merely appear to be asleep. It had fooled the handyman she had employed to come in and build a fire for her each day. When the gentleman entered Julia's home at eleven in the morning, he believed she was sleeping. He explained to law enforcement officers that he was quiet as he went about his work and left when the job was done. A search of the modest home Julia rented revealed that many of her possessions were missing. The citizens of Virginia City were outraged by the crime.

Julia Bulette was born in London, England, in 1832. She arrived in Virginia City in 1863. Men in the bustling silver mining community supported a number of sporting women, and Julia was no exception. She was an independent contractor. She did not work as a madam of a house of ill repute, managing other women in the trade. She had a number of regular customers, including Thomas Peasley. Peasley owned a local saloon and was known to be Julia's favorite paramour. In addition to running a business, Peasley was a volunteer firefighter. Julia's interest in the Virginia Engine Company Number One began with him. She supported the crew monetarily when she could and cheered them on whenever they were called to a job. In recognition of her service, she was presented with a handsome feminine rendition of a fireman's uniform. It consisted of a fireman's shield, front shirt, belt, and helmet embossed with the insignia of Virginia Engine Company Number One. Julia was the only woman who was an honorary member of the volunteer force.

The murder of the well-liked courtesan baffled many. She owned a few beautiful gowns but did not have an extensive wardrobe; nor did she have any jewelry of great worth. The home where she lived was furnished with items of good quality but was not opulent. Julia's estate was worth $875.43. She owed more than $790 in unpaid bills, including $291 in legal fees and an outstanding balance for alcohol she kept on hand for her customers. She generally served whiskey and brandy but had bottles of ale, port, claret, and rum available as well.

An auction of Julia's belongings was held on March 28, 1868. Her friend Mary J. Minnivie was the administrator of her estate and provided a list of the deceased's personal property. It consisted of the following: one blue plaid silk dress; one red moiré antique dress and bodice; a black silk dress; one purple dress; one silk cap rimmed with fur; one blue flannel shirt; one silver cup marked J. C. B.; one pair red silk stockings; three chemises; one white silk chord; four handkerchiefs; one pair of gloves; one brown silk necktie; one fur cape; one fur collar; four fur muffs; one purple hood; one porte-monnaie (a small pocketbook or purse); one gold hunting watch, a gold chain, and charms; one watch case; one jet-set breast pin, earrings, and cross; and one silver brick marked "Julia."

The sale of Julia's things did not cover all she owed when she died. Her creditors would have to settle for whatever they were given toward the unpaid bills.

Virginia City police conducted an intense search for Julia's murderer, but four months after her body had been discovered, authorities still had no leads. It appeared as though the unknown assailant had fled the area and any hope of ever finding the perpetrator had ended. According to the November 9, 1955, edition of the *Reno Gazette*, it wasn't until Mrs. Cazentre, wife of the owner of a small restaurant in Gold Hill, Nevada, stumbled upon a clue to the crime that the police investigation was renewed.

In April 1867 Mrs. Cazentre was looking over a fine piece of silk she was going to use to make a dress when two customers came into the restaurant for breakfast, sat down at a table, and began talking. Their discussion centered on Julia Bulette's brutal murder and the failure of the authorities to find her killer. Mrs. Cazentre overheard the customers mention that the murderer was believed to have stolen two pieces of silk dress material from his victim. Mrs. Cazentre was astonished. A few months prior to this occasion she had purchased material from a drifter for an incredibly modest price. When she bought the fabric, Mrs. Cazentre asked the salesman how he came to have such a fine piece of material, and the man told her it had once belonged to a lady whose husband had been killed in a mining accident.

After Mrs. Cazentre finished speaking with the two customers, she hurried out of the restaurant to the courthouse with the material in tow. She shared everything that had transpired with Judge Jesse S. Pitzer. He

The beloved Julia Bulette proudly poses for the camera dressed in her volunteer firefighter's garb.

JULIA BULETTE

then summoned Harry and Sam Rosner, owners of a local mercantile called Rosner and Company, who identified Mrs. Cazentre's silk as the material sold to Julia. Judge Pitzer then suggested that Mrs. Cazentre view all the drifters, vagabonds, and thugs currently in jail for vagrancy to see if the man who had sold her the silk might be among them. It turned out the salesman was indeed incarcerated at the city jail, and Mrs. Cazentre quickly identified him.

The culprit was a Frenchman named John Millian who had been employed at a bakery in town. In March 1867 Millian had attempted to attack one of Julia's neighbors. He had broken into the neighbor's home carrying a knife. When the woman screamed he had run. The neighbor had reported the attack to the police and led them through Virginia City in search of Millian. He had been arrested trying to leave town. After Mrs. Cazentre identified Millian within his jail cell, authorities examined a trunk Millian's employer said belonged to him that was stored at the bakery. The trunk was full of Julia's possessions. Once he was presented with the evidence against him, Millian confessed to the crime. He withdrew his confession shortly after his trial began on July 2, 1867.

According to Alfred Doten, editor of the *Gold Hill News,* the court proceedings "created great excitement in the city." A myriad of witnesses were called to the stand to testify against Millian, including Mrs. Cazentre, who told her story about the material. The proprietors of Rosner and Company explained the fabric was purchased at their store, and Gertrude Holmes identified Julia's belongings found in Millian's trunk.

Charles Dlong, a Virginia City attorney and one-time California state assemblyman, represented Millian. He argued that his client did not murder Julia. He claimed she was killed by two other men and that Millian was asked to store the possessions for them. Millian told the court he did not know the names of the actual killers and could not produce witnesses to support his claim. The case was handed over to the jury eight hours after opening statements had been made. They found Millian guilty of murder and he was sentenced to be hanged. All attempts for appeals were denied. On April 24, 1868, Millian was taken from the jail and loaded aboard a carriage. Surrounded by the National Guard and armed deputies, he was driven to the gallows a mile outside town.

According to the June 9, 1868, edition of the *Janesville Gazette*, so many had gathered to watch the hanging that it was difficult for the carriage to make it down the street. The article read:

Only by scolding, pushing and threatening with a bayonet was there enough room to proceed. The road to the gallows was lined on either side with men, women and children, all striving with open mouths and distended eyes to catch a glimpse of the prisoner. A way in advance, as far as the eye could see a mob of men, women and children were hurrying along the road, over the hills, and across lots and fields in the direction of the spot fixed upon for the execution.

It was a motley crowd: white women with children in their arms, Piute squaws with young ones upon their backs, long-tailed and wide-eyed Chinese men, women of the town and women evidently from the country, with men of all kinds and colors. Here was calculated a crowd of not less than three thousand persons.

Although he wore a somewhat haggard look from his long confinement, yet Millian showed he possessed nerves of steel. He read his manuscript which was quite lengthy, in a loud and clear voice, and held the paper so firmly in his hands that not the slightest tremor was observable. Having finished reading, he spoke for some two to three minutes in the French language, when he turned about and shook hands with the sheriff and kissed the reverend fathers. He then stepped to the front of the scaffold and, in very good English said, "Mr. Hall and family, I am very much obliged to you for your services, and also to the kind ladies that visited me in my cell."

Two young men of the Hall family then went upon the scaffold and shook hands with him. His arms and legs were now firmly pinioned, himself taking off his slippers and otherwise assisting, his collar opened and the fatal noose adjusted around his neck by the under Sheriff. He took one last look at the noose as it was brought forward, then stood while it was being properly placed, with his eyes downcast and his lips moving as though uttering a prayer.

The black cap was now pulled down over his face, and on the instant the under Sheriff detached the fastening of the trap, and the body of Millian disappeared through the scaffold. He fell between six and seven feet and was doubtless killed instantly, as his neck was dislocated.

Sagebrush and erosion have almost obscured the spot at Flower Hill Cemetery believed to be the last resting place of Julia Bulette. The wooden marker at her grave, as well as the fence surrounding the plot, has a reddish tint due to weathering. Nobody ever recorded where exactly Julia was buried. The proper citizens of Virginia City preferred to forget it.

Alice Ivers

Deadwood Cardsharp

"It was the damnedest faro game I ever saw. The game seesawed back and forth with Alice always picking up the edge; a few times it terminated only long enough for the player to eat a sandwich and wash it down with a boiler maker."

GAMBLER MARION SPEER'S COMMENTS ON THE POKER GAME
BETWEEN ALICE IVERS AND JACK HARDESTY, 1872

A steady stream of miners, ranchers, and cowhands filtered in and out of the Number 10 Saloon in Deadwood, South Dakota. An inexperienced musician playing an out-of-tune accordion squeezed out a familiar melody, ushering the pleasure seekers inside. Burlap curtains were pulled over the dusty windows, and fans that hung down from the ceiling turned lazily.

A distressed mahogany bar stood alongside one wall of the business, and behind it was a surly looking bartender. He was splashing amber liquid into glasses as fast as he could. A row of tables and chairs occupied the area opposite the bar. Every seat was filled with a card player. Among the seat of male gamblers was one woman; everyone called her Poker Alice.

She was an alarming beauty, fair-skinned and slim. She had one eye on the cards she was dealing and another on the men at the game two tables down.

Warren G. Tubbs was studying the cards in his hand so intently he didn't notice the hulk of a man next to him get up and walk around behind him. The huge man with massive shoulders and ham-like hands that hung low to his sides peered over Tubbs's shoulder and scowled down at the mountain of chips before him. Alice's intensely blue eyes carefully watched the brute's actions. He casually reached back at his belt and produced a sharp knife from the leather sheath hanging off his waist. Just as he was about to plunge the weapon into Tubbs's back, a gunshot rang out.

A sick look filled the man's face, and the frivolity in the saloon came to a halt. He slowly dropped the knife. Before dropping to his knees, he turned in the direction from which the bullet had come. Alice stared back at him, her .38 pistol pointed at his head. The man fell face first onto the floor. His dead body was quickly removed to make way for another player. In a matter of minutes, the action inside the tavern returned to normal. Tubbs caught Alice's gaze and grinned. He nodded to her and waggled his fingers in a kind of salute. She smiled slightly and turned her attention wholly back to the poker game in front of her.

Alice Ivers never sat down to play poker without holding at least one gun. She generally carried a pistol in her dress pocket, and often she also had a backup weapon in her purse. The frontier was rough and wild, and wearing a gun, particularly while playing cards, was a matter of survival. It was a habit for Poker Alice.

She was born on February 17, 1851, in Sudbury, Devonshire, England. Alice's father, whom some historians indicate was a teacher while others maintain he was a lawyer, brought his wife and family to the United States in 1863. They settled first in Virginia and later moved to Fort Meade, South Dakota.

Like most people at the time, the Iverses were lured west by gold. No matter what gold rush town she was living in, Alice always attended school. She was a bright young girl who excelled in math. The yellow-haired, precocious child quickly grew into a handsome woman, attracting the attention of every eligible bachelor in the area. Frank Duffield, a mining engineer, won her heart and hand. After the two married he escorted his bride to Lake City, where he was employed. The southwestern Colorado silver camp was an unrefined, isolated location with very little to offer in terms of entertainment.

With the exception of watching the cardsharps and high-hatted gamblers make a fortune off the luckless miners, there was nothing but work to occupy time.

Bored with life as a simple homemaker and undaunted by convention, Alice visited the gambling parlors. Her husband and his friends taught her how to play a variety of poker games, and in no time she became an exceptional player. The fact that she was a mathematical genius added tremendously to her talent.

Most every night Alice was seated at the faro table of the Gold Dust Gambling House, dealing cards and challenging fast-talking thrill seekers to "put their money into circulation." She won the majority of the hands she played, whether it was five-card draw, faro, or blackjack. Her days of gambling for pleasure alone came to an end when Frank was killed in a mining accident. Left with no viable means of support, Alice decided to turn her hobby into a profession.

Some well-known gamblers, like Jack "Lucky" Hardesty, were not as accepting of a woman cardsharp as others. He made his thoughts on the subject plainly known one evening when he sat down at a faro table and glanced across the green felt at Alice. He refused to play against her, insisting that faro was a man's game. Alice didn't shy away from the verbal assault.

She calmly conveyed her intention to remain at the table until he dealt her a hand. Hardesty eventually gave in, but, before he let her have any cards, he warned her not to cry when she lost to him. Poker Alice simply grinned.

At the end of the night, Hardesty was out everything. Alice had won more than $1,500 off him and the other men who wagered on the game. Curious onlookers were reported to have remarked that he had "lost his money like he had a hole in his pocket as big as a stove pipe." Hardesty attributed Alice's numerous wins to luck alone.

Alice took that so-called luck from Colorado to other gambling spots in Arizona, Oklahoma, Kansas, Texas, New Mexico, and South Dakota. Along the way the fashionable beauty developed a habit of smoking cigars and a taste for alcohol. Wherever the stakes were high, the whiskey smooth, and the smokes free, that's where Alice would be. She generally said nothing if she won, but if she lost a hand, she'd blurt out, "Goddamnit!"

The name Poker Alice meant increased business for gaming houses. People flocked to see the highly skilled poker player "packing a heavy load of luck" and puffing on a thin, black stogie. Warren G. Tubbs was one of

Alice Ivers, better known as Poker Alice, was one of the best known renegade lady gamblers in the West. She was a master card player who at one time dealt cards to Wild Bill Hickok and Calamity Jane. Her "poker face" or deadpan expression was her winning advantage.

the many who came to see Alice play cards. Warren was a house painter and part-time gambler.

He was captivated by her, so much so he didn't mind losing a hand or two to her. She found him equally charming, and after a brief courtship the pair married.

Alice was the better card player of the two and was the primary financial supporter for the family. Tubbs continued with his painting business but would not give up the game entirely. The couple spent many evenings playing poker at the same parlor. Whatever Warren lost, Alice made up for in substantial winnings. The average night's win for her was more than $200.

Alice's reputation preceded her. To every town the pair traveled, she was offered $25 a night, plus a portion of her winnings to act as dealer for the gaming parlor. Alice and Warren were bringing in large amounts of money and spending just as much. Alice made frequent visits to New York, where she would purchase the finest clothes and jewels, attend several theatrical performances and musicals, and lavish her friends with expensive gifts. When the cash ran out, she would return to her husband and her cards and begin rebuilding her bank.

Poker Alice was very protective of her husband and got him out of trouble many times. Warren drank to excess and frequently started fights. Alice would end any squabble that threatened his life.

Sober, Warren might have been faster on the draw against an offended cowhand. Alice was the better shot most of the time. Her father taught her how to shoot using his Starr Army .44 revolver. By the age of twelve, she was as fast and accurate with the weapon as any boy her age. When she got older and there were lulls between poker games, Alice would practice her marksmanship by shooting knobs off the frames of pictures hanging on the walls. Her proficiency with a gun was proof to anyone who thought of crossing her or Warren that she could handle herself.

In 1874 Warren and Alice made their way to New Mexico. They had heard that the poker tables in Silver City were some of the richest in the country. Within hours of their arrival, Alice joined in a faro game. Hand after hand, she raked in piles of chips. Saloon patrons pressed in around the game to watch the brilliant blonde win again and again. Before the sun rose the following morning, Alice had broken the bank and added to her holdings an estimated $150,000.

Alice and Warren followed the gold rush riches to the town of Deadwood, South Dakota. There they hoped to continue increasing their winnings. Her expert card playing and beautiful East Coast gowns brought gamblers to her table. Residents referred to her as the "Faro Queen of Deadwood."

Whenever Wild Bill Hickok was around, he liked to play against the Queen. In fact, he had invited her to sit in on a hand with him on August 2, 1876, the day Jack McCall shot and killed the legendary western character. Alice had declined, stating that she was already committed to another game. When she heard he'd been killed, she raced to the scene. Hickok was sprawled out on the floor, and McCall was running for his life. Looking down at her friend's body, she sadly said, "Poor Wild Bill. He was sitting where I would have been if I'd played with him."

In 1910 Alice and Warren celebrated thirty-four years of marriage. Together they had won and lost a fortune, bought and sold several ranches in Colorado and South Dakota, and raised seven children. In the winter of that year, Warren contracted pneumonia and died. Alice remarried less than a year later. Her new husband was an obnoxious drunk named George Huckert; he died on their third wedding anniversary.

At this point in her long life, Poker Alice had rid herself of the fashionable dress she once subscribed to and took to wearing khaki skirts, men's shirts, and an old campaign hat. Her beauty had all but faded, and her hair had turned silver.

The only thing that remained of the Alice of old was her habit of smoking cigars.

After moving back and forth from Deadwood to Rapid City and back again, Poker Alice left Deadwood for good in 1913. She relocated to Sturgis, South Dakota, and bought a home a few miles from Fort Meade. She also purchased a profitable "entertainment" business, one that attracted hordes of soldiers stationed at the post. In addition to female companionship, she sold bootleg whiskey.

At the age of sixty-two, Poker Alice found her talent with a gun to still be useful. When a pair of soldiers started fighting and breaking up her house, she stepped in with her .38 pistol to stop the ruckus. The chaos ended in the death of one of the men and the arrest of Alice Tubbs. She was charged with murder but was later acquitted on the grounds of justifiable homicide.

Alice's health began deteriorating after the arrest. She was wracked with pain throughout her body. Physicians informed her that the problem was her gall bladder and that it had to be removed. She was told that the surgery was risky for a woman of her age. Alice, who thrived on risk, decided to go through with the operation.

On February 27, 1930, three weeks after having surgery, Alice passed away. Her estate, which was at one time estimated to be worth millions, had been reduced to $50 and a few possessions. Poker Alice was buried in the Sturgis Catholic Cemetery. She was seventy-nine when she died.

Jennie Rogers

Queen of the Denver Row

"Each afternoon at about three o'clock, the August lawmakers would retire to Jennie Rogers' palace of joy on Market Street and there disport themselves in riotous fashion . . ."

ROCKY MOUNTAIN NEWS, 1890

A blood orange sun shone down on the dusty, main thoroughfare in Denver, Colorado. Miners and townspeople scurried about with their daily activities, pausing every so often to talk with friends and acquaintances. A sudden commotion at the end of the street drew attention away from their regular routine. An open, horse-drawn coach carrying a host of overly painted girls rolled into the bustling mining camp. The bawdy cargo drew stares and disapproving gasps from respectable women.

Jennie Rogers, a tall, attractive madam and self-proclaimed Queen of the Colorado Underworld, steered the rig slowly past the shops and saloon. The raven-haired woman was dressed in a green velvet dress and wore a beautiful pair of emerald earrings. The other fancily dressed ladies in the coach waved at the gathering crowd lining the streets.

Cowpunchers, miners, and outlaws shouted out their approval as they carefully eyed the stunning parade of women.

The prostitutes' U-shaped, low-cut bodices showed enough of their youthfully solid and well-rounded necks and breasts to be an enticement. It was exactly the kind of response Jennie hoped to provoke. Amorous men followed the coach to a parlor house on Market Street and there, history records, "a good time was had by all."

Denver's red-light district in 1880 was a busy area. Prospectors had invaded the area some thirty years prior, and the discovery of gold there sparked an influx of miners and their families. By the time Jennie arrived on the scene in 1879, the gold camp had become a booming city with a network of railroads and a variety of profitable industries in place. Madams converged on the growing Colorado Territory to amass their own fortunes with a service many lonely men believed was a necessary evil.

Madam Rogers's two-story brick brothel was a popular stop for those living in or passing through the region. It was furnished with enamel and brass beds and hand-carved dressers, desks, and chairs and decorated with lace curtains and imported rugs. The house was a lavish oasis for its rough guests.

It was precisely the type of establishment Jennie envisioned owning when she entered the business in her twenties.

Born in Allegheny, Pennsylvania, on the Fourth of July, 1843, her given name was Leah. Her father, James Weaver, was a poor farmer. When she was old enough, Jennie helped make ends meet by selling the family's homegrown produce in the street markets of Pittsburgh. Her natural good looks prompted many men to propose marriage. It wasn't until G. Friess, a prominent physician in the area, proposed that she agreed to marry.

Dr. Friess's practice kept him away from home quite often, and his very social wife was left at home alone. In a short time Jennie tired of the solitary life and left the marriage.

Yearning for adventure, Jennie took off with the captain of a steamship and traveled the waterways between Pennsylvania and Ohio. After several years of living on the river, the lifestyle lost its luster. She abandoned the relationship in favor of working as a housekeeper on dry land.

Jennie took a position as a domestic at the Pittsburgh mayor's home in the mid-1870s. The mayor's constituency was outraged that he would allow a woman with such questionable morals to work in his house. Jennie spoke openly about her affairs, and when news that she had left two men reached the public at large, they were against her as a hire. The mayor let her go, but not before advancing her a substantial amount of money to back a business she had in mind to start in St. Louis, Missouri.

Historians have no idea why Jennie chose to pursue a career as a madam. She was an astute businesswoman, and, given that fact, she must have intuitively known the money to be made in arranging company for needy men. Whatever the reason, her first parlor house in St. Louis was a huge success. Many laborers and business magnates flocked to her "fashionable resort."

When news of a gold strike in Colorado reached Jennie, she decided to travel west to the Mile High City to consider opening a second parlor house. After seeing the flood of humanity that had descended upon Denver and calculating how much money there was to be made, she decided to purchase another brothel. Jennie paid $4,600 for the house, and in less than a month she had made back her investment.

Jennie's Denver business was located in a section of town known as the Row. Similar houses stood next to hers and were run by some of the most famous madams of the time. Mattie Silks, Laura Evans, and Lizzie Preston all had successful businesses in the same location.

Not everyone appreciated the services Jennie and the other women had to offer. It is rumored that an outcry of respectable citizens demanded the city council take action against the numerous "dens of iniquity." In an effort to shame the madams into shutting their houses down, the council ordered that all "women of ill repute" wear yellow ribbons. Undaunted by the attempt to humiliate them, Jennie and the other madams decided to dress in yellow from head to toe. Their dresses, shoes, and parasols were yellow and their hats were decorated with large yellow plumes. Their defiant display drew a lot of attention and eventually forced the council to rescind the order.

Four years after opening the Denver parlor house, Jennie had earned enough money to build a new brothel. To handle her increased business, she built an opulent three-story home with fifteen rooms. The spacious house, which contained three parlors, a ballroom, dining room, large kitchen, wine cellar, and servants' quarters, was lavishly decorated. The numerous clients that frequented the spectacular residence proclaimed Jennie to be the Queen of the Row.

Law enforcement officers visited Jennie's new place on a regular basis. She was fined several times for keeping a "noisy and disorderly house."

Patrons were arrested for morphine use, and a handful of Jennie's girls were apprehended for stealing property from the men who hired them. The constant trouble the parlor houses and their residents caused prompted a second public outcry against the bordellos on the Row in

Though appearing demure in this studio portrait, Jennie Rogers declared herself
"Queen of the Colorado Underworld."

1886. Politicians and townspeople were again demanding the houses be shut down. For a period of six months, officials raided the brothels, issuing fines and arresting uncooperative prostitutes.

According to a report in the August 12, 1886, edition of the *Denver Times*, "The last few nights the police have been busily occupied among the houses of infamy, 'pulling' those institutions, and the result has been quite an increase in the sum paid over by the police court to the city treasury."

Jennie Rogers and fourteen other prominent madams were arrested for "keeping lewd houses." All were found guilty and fined $75. Undeterred by the incident, Jennie and her competition were back in operation days after the raids.

Madam Rogers's insatiable appetite for the finer things drove her to some unsavory actions. With the help of one of her many lovers, she concocted a drunken, murderous scandal to blackmail a politician and parlor house regular.

Jennie threatened to go public with the information she'd put together. The man was so convinced he might be guilty he agreed to pay her $17,000 to keep her quiet.

Jennie used the ill-gotten gain to build a magnificent brick and stone house. The grand brothel, which opened for business in 1889, was the talk of the West. The ceiling-to-floor mirrors that covered the walls in the reception hall were the topic of conversation from Denver to San Francisco. The unique bordello was nicknamed the "House of Mirrors." Crystal chandeliers, oriental rugs, marble tables, and grand pianos were a few of the other luxurious features.

The women Madam Rogers hired to work at her place were well groomed, had the most current hairstyles, and possessed a level of sophistication and manner not found in the average parlor house. They were also adorned in the finest fashions. Dressmakers would bring samples of their work for Jennie to see. She would select the garments each employee was to wear, and the cost came out of that employee's pay. The care Jennie took to present a high-class product ensured a clientele of the same refinement. Senators and legislators held meetings in the general proximity of the House of Mirrors so they could stop by Jennie's place for a visit after work.

When Jennie wasn't laboring at her trade, she was spending time with her stable of horses. She was an expert rider and could handle a coach better than most professional drivers. During one of her many weekend shopping sprees and subsequent trips to the Tabor Grand Opera House, she noticed a gruff young hack driver watching her every move. John A. Wood was a twenty-three-year-old who had worked around horses all his life. He was moved by Jennie's kind treatment of the animals and her ability to manage a coach. He introduced himself to her, and they became fast friends.

John was a poor man, lacking in pretension, and Jennie found that aspect of his personality irresistible. She offered to better his circumstances by purchasing a saloon for him to manage. Her sincere concern for his well-being made him fall in love with her. In a short time Jennie had fallen in love with him as well.

In the spring of 1887, Jennie opened a saloon in Salt Lake City, Utah. Researchers at the Denver Historical Society speculate that the location was chosen in an attempt to keep Jennie's professional life as a madam and private life with her lover as separate as possible.

The Utah saloon was a huge success almost from the moment the doors swung open. Jennie was pleased with the way John handled the tavern and made frequent trips to oversee the operation and spend time with him. Most of her trips were planned well in advance, but on one occasion she decided to surprise her lover with an unscheduled visit. When Jennie entered John's living quarters, she found him with another woman. Enraged by the betrayal, Jennie pulled a pistol from a pocket in the folds of her gown and shot him. John's wounds were not fatal. The sheriff arrived on the scene, and Jennie was promptly arrested. When John was able, he told the authorities that Jennie's actions were justifiable, and she was released.

Jennie returned to Denver with a renewed commitment to bettering her already flourishing parlor houses and adding to her holdings. Using the profits made from her brothels, Madam Rogers purchased several acres of premium land in the northern portion of town. She also purchased several shares in an irrigation and reservoir project. The investment eventually yielded a tidy sum.

In spite of her increased riches and thriving businesses, Jennie was not happy. She was haunted by the image of the man she loved in the arms of another woman.

The abrupt end of their relationship had not relieved her of the affection she still harbored for John. By the time Jennie was forty-five, two years had passed since she had seen him, but she still thought of him often and wondered how he was doing. She sank into a deep depression over her lost love, deeply regretting her actions. Visits from famous friends and architects, like William Quayle of San Diego and Marshall Field of Chicago, did nothing to improve her melancholy state.

In May 1889 Jennie received news of John's whereabouts, and her spirits were finally lifted. He was operating a saloon in Omaha, Nebraska. He had never married, and it was known by his many friends and acquaintances that he was still in love with Jennie. Jennie swallowed her pride and wrote John a letter, hoping beyond hope that he would respond. He did, and the two began a regular correspondence. By midsummer the two were reunited and altar bound. They were married on August 13, 1889. Eight years after they exchanged vows, John Wood died from unknown causes. Jennie was devastated. She laid his body to rest in Denver's Fairmont Cemetery under a massive tombstone that simply reads, "He is not dead, but sleeping."

Jennie drowned her sorrows in her work. An influx of new brothels was siphoning business away from the House of Mirrors, and madams up and down the Row had taken out ads for their establishments in a publication called the *Denver Red Book: A Reliable Directory of the Pleasure Resorts of Denver*. Some of the houses hoped to entice clients with their offer of fine wines and cigars; others listed the number of elegant rooms they had. Jennie's advertisement was a simple one: It listed a name, an address, and the bold statement that everything was "first class."

Lonely, in poor health, and complacent about her long career in Colorado, Jennie eventually decided to lease out her parlor houses to other madams and move to the Midwest. Before she departed, her physician diagnosed her with chronic Bright's disease, an inflammation of the filtering unit in the kidneys. She had suffered with the condition for many years but had refused to do as her doctor recommended. The ailment was now in an advanced state, and she was strongly advised to move to a more agreeable climate.

In 1902 Jennie left the high altitude of Denver and headed to the lowlands around Chicago. Doctors ordered Jennie to stay in bed for at least seven months after she arrived, but she refused. Jennie believed the move was enough of a change for her health. She went right to work and purchased a large parlor house in the heart of Chicago.

She acquired the funds for the down payment by selling off some of her Denver property and her favorite emerald earrings. In no time the new bordello was busy, and money was coming in at a rapid pace.

Just as her health was improving and her heart was on the mend, she met a charming thirty-seven-year-old contractor who captivated her. Archibald T. Fitzgerald was not an overly handsome man. He had dark features, a double chin, and a receding hairline, but he showered Jennie with the attention she was craving. Their courtship was brief, but in that time Jennie fell deeply in love with Archibald. Archibald fell deeply in love with Jennie's money.

Archibald abused the influence he had over Jennie, encouraging her to spend her fortune on expensive carriages and trips to Hot Springs, Arkansas. He convinced her that the medicinal qualities in the hot springs would bring about an instant cure for Bright's disease. Blinded by his charisma, Jennie quickly accepted his offer of marriage after he presented her with a diamond and ruby engagement ring, a ring that was more than likely paid for with Madam Rogers's own money. Archibald and Jennie exchanged vows at Hot Springs on April 26, 1904.

Six months after the Fitzgeralds said "I do," Jennie learned that Archibald was a bigamist. He had two other wives besides Jennie: one in Kansas City, Missouri, and the other across town in Chicago. Jennie considered divorcing Archibald several times, but he always managed to talk her out of it. The longer she stayed with him, the more money he spent. In five years Jennie was near bankruptcy.

Consumed with worry over her finances, and preoccupied with maintaining her parlor houses in Colorado and Illinois, as well as dealing with her fragile marriage, Jennie finally succumbed to poor health. She was taken to a hospital, but nothing could be done to revive her. Uremic poisoning had attacked her kidneys. Her funeral was attended by most of the madams from the Row and several of her employees and business associates. Archibald Fitzgerald was conspicuous by his absence.

The Queen of the Denver Row was secretly buried next to her second husband. The marking on her tombstone reads, "Leah J. Wood. Died October 17, 1909." She was sixty-six years old.

Eleanora Dumont

The Twenty-One Dealer

"The Dumont woman was vanity itself. Vain, moustached, always making airs."

SAN FRANCISCO ACTOR JOHN HENRY ANDERSON, 1869

A pair of miners squinted into the early morning sky as they rode out of the gold town of Bodie, California, toward their claim. Shafts of light poked through scattered clouds a few miles ahead on the rocky road. In the near distance the men spotted what looked like a bundle of clothing lying just out of reach of the sun's tentacles. They speculated that some prospector must have lost his gear riding through the area, but as they approached the item, it was clear that it was not simply a stray pack. A woman's body lay drawn in a fetal position, dead. The curious miners dismounted and hurried over to the unfortunate soul.

The vacant eyes that stared up at the men were those of the famed Eleanora Dumont, "the Blackjack Queen of the Northern Mines." An empty bottle of poison rested near her lifeless frame, and her dusty face was streaked with dried tears. One of the miners covered her with a blanket from his bedroll while the other eyed the vultures circling overhead.

Misfortune and a broken heart led to the fifty-year-old Dumont's downfall. At one time she had been the toast of the gold rush and one of the most desirable women in the West. A string of bad luck in love and cards drove her to take her own life.

Eleanora Dumont was born in New Orleans in 1829 and came to San Francisco in the early 1850s. She proudly proclaimed to all who asked that she "did not make the long journey for love of the frontier or to find the man of her dreams." She wanted wealth. "The western heartthrob I'm after is not a man, but that glittery rock lying among the foothills of the Gold Country," she confessed.

People of every kind and description poured into San Francisco bringing tents, building shacks, and sleeping on the ground under blankets draped over poles. Men leapt from ships fired with the urge to get into the gold fields and find the mother lode. They congregated with the miners who had found gold and come to town to spend it. There was a wild gambling fever in the air. Eleanora capitalized on the fever by working as a dealer at a saloon called the Bella Union. Hardworking prospectors stood in line to lose their chunks of gold to the stunningly beautiful and demure young woman.

Within a few months Eleanora had earned enough money to invest in her own gambling den. In 1854 she boarded a stage bound for Nevada City, the richest gold town in California, and purchased a vacant storefront to turn into a gaming house. She called herself Madam Dumont and invited thrill seekers to take her on in a game of twenty-one or blackjack.

Her establishment was tastefully decorated and furnished with expensive chairs and settees, carpets, and gas chandeliers. Her resort was open twenty-four hours a day, and patrons were offered free champagne. Even though customers were required to clean off their boots before entering and were ordered to keep their language clean as well, Dumont's place soon became the favorite spot for thirsty gold miners and other characters passing through.

A big part of the attraction was Madam Dumont's superb card playing. She excelled in the game she referred to as *vingt-et-un*, or blackjack. The object of the game was to accumulate cards with a higher count than that of the dealer but not exceeding twenty-one.

Not everyone approved of a woman operating a gaming house. Dumont was frequently chastised by elite political and social influences in Nevada City. She ignored their remarks and the remarks of the men who lost to her, but she never turned away a customer who insinuated she was a cheat or challenged her to a game. Dutch Carver was a prospector who did just that.

Late one summer evening, the drunken Carver burst into Madam Dumont's house and demanded to see her. "I'm here for a fling at the cards tonight with your lady boss," Carver told one of the scantily attired women who worked at the parlor. He handed the young lady a silver dollar and smiled confidently. "Now, you take this and buy yourself a drink. Come around after I clean out the Madam, and maybe we'll do some celebrating." The woman laughed in Carver's face. "I won't hold my breath," she said.

Eleanora soon appeared at the gambling table dressed in a stylish garibaldi blouse and skirt. She sat down across from Carver and began shuffling the deck of cards. "What's your preference?" she asked him. Carver laid a wad of money out on the table in front of him. "I don't care," he said. "I've got more than $200 here. Let's get going now, and I don't want to quit until you've got all my money, or until I've got a considerable amount of yours." She smiled and obligingly began dealing the cards. In a short hour and a half, Dutch Carver had lost his entire bankroll to Madam Dumont.

When the game ended the gambler stood up and started to leave the saloon. Dumont ordered him to sit down and have a drink on the house. He took a place at the bar, and the bartender served him a glass of milk. This was a customary course of action at Eleanora's house. All losers had to partake. Madam Dumont believed that "any man silly enough to lose his last cent to a woman deserved a milk diet."

Dumont's reputation as a cardsharp spread throughout the foothills of the Gold Country. No one had ever seen a successful woman dealer before. Gaming establishments were dominated by men. Dealing cards and operating a faro table was considered a man's job, and there was not a lot of respectability associated with the position. Eleanor defied convention and proved that the appearance of a beautiful woman behind the gambling table was good business. Curious gamblers from Wyoming to Texas flocked to the club to watch the trim blackjack queen with the nimble fingers shuffle the deck. Rival saloons found it necessary to hire women just to keep up with the competition.

Eleanora's success and beauty attracted many young men. Historical records indicate that several men fell hopelessly in love with the fair Miss Dumont. They proposed marriage and had their hearts broken when she refused. Dell Fallon was one such suitor whose affections she rejected. He popped the question to her one night while sitting across from her at a blackjack table. "Madam Eleanora," he began, "I know I

Eleanora Dumont, aka Madam Mustache, was unafraid to use her pistol to defend herself.

ain't worthy to ask the question. But would you consent to become my wife?"

"My friend," Eleanora gently replied, "I am grateful that you hold me in such high regard. But I am not free to follow the dictates of my heart. I must go alone."

Eleanora could have had men by the score, but her heart was set on just one: Editor Wait of the *Nevada Journal*. She adored him and longed for the respectability he offered. Wait never returned her feelings. He did not want to be involved with someone lacking in social standing. Her broken heart over the matter would never really heal. To get through the hurt and rejection, she set her sights on building a bigger gambling casino on the main street of town.

In less than a year after her arrival in the Gold Country, Eleanora had amassed a considerable fortune. Her business continued to grow, and she found she needed to take on a partner to assist with the daily operation of the club. She teamed up with a professional gambler from New York named David Tobin. Together they opened a larger establishment where Tobin attended the games of faro and keno.

Business was good for a couple of years, but by 1856 the gold mines had stopped producing the precious metal, and Eleanora and Tobin decided to dissolve their partnership and move on. Madam Dumont had more than financial reasons for wanting to leave the area. When she found out that Editor Wait was sharing his time with a young woman he planned to marry, she was devastated. Before she left town she went to see him at the paper. Tears welled in her eyes as she kissed him lightly on the cheek. "I'm leaving Nevada City to forget," she told him. "I hope you have a good life."

Eleanora took her winnings to the rich gold camps of Columbia, California. She set up her table in the hotel, and when profits slowed down she moved on to yet another mining community. She had a reputation for being honest and generous to the losers, and many times she loaned the miners a few dollars to gamble with.

By the time she reached the age of thirty, her good looks had started to fade. The facial hair that grew under her nose earned her the nickname "Madam Mustache."

She decided to use the money she had earned to get out of the gambling business altogether and buy a cattle ranch near Carson City, Nevada. The work was hard, and Eleanora knew next to nothing about animals and even less about ranching. She was lonely, out of her element, and desperate. That's when she met Jack McKnight. "I knew when I met him that he was the answer to my prayers," she confessed. "He was just what I needed and at the right time."

Jack claimed to be a cattle buyer, and he swept Eleanora off her feet. He was actually a scoundrel who made his living off the misfortunes of others. He was handsome, a smooth talker, and very well dressed. The two married shortly after they met. Eleanora married for love. Jack married for money and property. Eleanora trusted him and turned everything she had over to him.

They had been married less than a month when Jack deserted her, taking all her money with him. He had also sold her ranch and left her with all of his outstanding debts. Eleanora was crushed.

Alone and destitute, she was forced to return to the mining camps and take up gambling again. She had been away from the blackjack table for more than a year. She wasn't as good a card player as she once was, but she was still a fascination to most. They would come from miles around to hear her stories and to play a hand with the notorious Madam Mustache.

Eleanora took her blackjack game to many backwater towns across the West. She lost more hands than she won, and she began to earn most of her money as a prostitute and started drinking heavily as a way to deal with her tragic life.

At the age of fifty, she settled in the rough and wicked gold mining town of Bodie, California. Bodie had a reputation for violence. Shootings, stabbings, and thefts took place every day. The lady gambler, now frequently intoxicated, set up a blackjack table in one of the saloons there. Professional gamblers took Eleanora on, eventually leaving her penniless. She always had a smile for the men who fleeced her.

One night, after losing yet another hand, she drank down a glass of whiskey and excused herself from the table. The saloon patrons watched her leave the building and stagger off down Main Street. That was the last Madam Mustache was seen alive. Her body was found on an early September morning in 1879. The *Bodie Daily Free Press* reported her demise in the September 8 evening edition: "A woman named Eleanora Dumont was found dead today about one mile out of town, having committed suicide. She was well known through all the mining camps. Let her many good qualities invoke leniency in criticizing her failings."

Among the personal items found on Eleanora's body was a letter she had written and placed in an envelope for mailing. The envelope, which was addressed to the citizens of Nevada City, was splotched with tearstains. The letter contained a request by Eleanora that she be permitted to be buried in the gold rush town where she opened her first gambling parlor. She wanted to be buried next to her one true love, Editor Wait.

Local townspeople were able to pool only enough money to bury Madam Dumont in the Bodie Cemetery. They gave her a proper burial and refused to let her be laid to rest in the outcast section of the graveyard.

Madam Harriet

A Curious Criminal Case

Prostitutes, by nature of their profession, often find themselves in trouble with the law. It was not uncommon for a nineteenth-century harlot to be accused of blackmail, theft, or even murder. Such was the case of a soiled dove in Northern California. The curious criminal proceedings were held before Justice John Anderson in 1852, and an article in an August edition of the *Union News* attempted to unravel the mystery for its readers:

> *A public woman, popularly known as "Old Harriet," kept a saloon on Broad Street, overlooking Deer Creek. She had a man who kept bar for her and did any necessary fighting. Opposite her establishment was a dance house. A man named Pat Berry was mining on the opposite side of Deer Creek at Gold Run. Owing to a recent freshet there were no bridges at the foot of the town, but a tree had been cleared of limbs and felled across it, over which foot passengers made their way. The stream was still high and raged among the naked boulders and logs which were then innocent of tailings.*
>
> *On Saturday Berry came over to town, having made some money during the week, and rigged himself out with an entire new buckle. He spent the evening until late at the dance house and then went over to Old Harriet's place, which was the last ever seen of him alive.*
>
> *In the course of the night a man in the neighborhood heard what he took to be a cry of "murder," but he may have been mistaken. Two or three days after, about six miles below Nevada, in an eddy in the creek, Berry's body was found, completely naked. On the forehead was a large, extravagated wound, the blood discoloration proving that this wound was given while the person was alive. Finding him in this condition led to search for previous traces of him; and it was discovered*

POST THIS LICENSE UP.

LICENSE FOR PROSTITUTION.

No. 14

TO ALL WHO SHALL SEE THESE PRESENTS—GREETING:

Know Ye, That whereas, *Buffalo Sue*

on the *10* day of *May 1876*, paid to the City Secretary the sum of Two Dollars and Fifty Cents ($2.50), being the license imposed on a PROSTITUTE, and otherwise complied with the regulations of the City Ordinances in this behalf.

Therefore, the said *Buffalo Sue* is hereby authorized and empowered to follow said occupation or business for the term of THREE MONTHS, from the *10* day of *May 1876*

In Testimony Whereof, I have hereunto set my hand and caused the Seal of the City to be affixed, at the Secretary's office, in said City, this *10* day of *May 1876*

Expires *10* day of *August 1876*

NOT TRANSFERABLE

In some areas, prostitutes were required to buy and post licenses.
AUTHOR'S COLLECTION

that he had passed the evening at the dance house, and then gone to Old Harriet's, where all further trace of him was lost.

Harriet and her fighting man were arrested and charged before the justice with murder. McConnell prosecuted and Sawyer defended. The examination lasted several days. The prosecution proved that Berry had money, traced his movements the night of his death, as herein stated, showed that the wound on his head must have been given while he was alive, and that it was made with some round, blunt weapon; that there was a pair of scales on Old Harriet's counter, and a large weight, which would produce such a wound; the condition of the body, with a new, strong suit of clothes entirely missing; which, it was contended it was impossible could be torn off by the stream, or at least, without greatly marring the body, which was intact, except the death wound on the head. The cry of murder was also proven, leaving a close knitted theory by the prosecution, well-sustained before the drowning. As to the missing clothes it was argued, though with less confidence, that they had been stripped off by the water, rocks and logs.

The case was so puzzling that the justice took it under advisement for several days. While he was considering it, two men walked the log

63

in company, when one of them pitched off and disappeared. Everybody turned out to find the body, but the search was unsuccessful for several days, when it was found in the eddy below the town from which Berry's body was taken. The head of the new victim was marked with the same kind of extravagated wound as that of the first one, but there were no other wounds on the body, and all his clothes were gone except his shirt, which was turned inside out and hung at the wrist. The case was at once reopened and this evidence of what might happen was submitted. When she heard the new testimony Old Harriet exclaimed: "The Lord has intervened to save an innocent woman!" Of course the accused went free.

Minnie Smith

A Violent Hand

"Luck never gives; it only lends."

ANCIENT PROVERB

A tall, hump-shouldered man with gray, bushy hair and a hangdog look on his long, lumpy face pulled a stack of chips from the middle of the poker table toward him. Minnie Smith, the gambler who had dealt the winning hand, scowled at the player as he collected his earnings. "You're sure packin' a heavy load of luck, friend," Minnie said in a low, clipped tone.

"Luck had nothing to do with it," the man replied.

"You may be right at that," Minnie snapped back. She pushed back from the table a bit and eyed the bullwhip curled in her lap.

The man gave her a sly grin, "You're not sore about losing?" he asked.

"No," Minnie responded calmly. "I get mighty sore about cheating though." A tense silence filled the air as Minnie and the gambler stared down each other.

In the split second it took the man to jump up and reach for his gun, Minnie had snapped her whip and disarmed him. As the weapon toppled out of his hand, a breastplate holdout that had been tucked inside his jacket sleeve dropped onto the floor.

The man looked on in horror as the face cards attached to the hidden pocket scattered around him.

"I hate a cheat," Minnie snarled. All eyes were on the dealer as she reared back and let the whip fly. After a few painful strikes, the man dropped to his knees and desperately tried to find cover from the continued beating. Minnie was relentless and finally had to be subdued by the other card players around her. The gambler was helped off the floor and escorted to the town doctor.

That kind of violent exchange wasn't unusual in the rowdy railroad town of Colorado City, Colorado, in 1887. What made the event unique, however, was that a woman was the aggressor. The public display further enhanced the quick-temper reputation of the madam and sometimes gambler Minnie Smith. There were very few in and around the area that hadn't heard of her.

Almost nothing is known about Minnie's formative years. The first historical recording of the hotheaded Smith occurred in 1886 in Colorado City. She was recognized throughout Colorado not only as Minnie Smith but also as Lou Eaton and Dirty Alice. She used different pseudonyms in the various locations across the state where she owned bordellos and saloons. Like many madams, Minnie felt the alternate handles gave her a sense of mystery that ultimately brought in business.

Customers who frequented her two-story parlor house on the south side of Colorado City were impressed with her card-playing skills and the way she ran the establishment. She always managed to hire the most exotic beauties to work for her and kept patrons entertained dealing cards in between visits with her employees. Minnie herself was reportedly unattractive. Residents described her as a "slender woman, not good looking and a vixen when aroused."

The numerous run-ins she had with the law could have been avoided if she'd been able to control her fiery temper. Her career was mired in arrests for disorderly conduct and assault. She took on anyone who crossed her, male or female. She nearly beat an attorney to death with the butt of a gun for the disparaging remarks he made about her profession.

On January 24, 1891, Minnie traveled to Denver to recruit ladies to work at her new brothel in Creede. While visiting the booming metropolis, she stopped into a tavern for a drink. As the evening wore on, she continued to consume more alcohol. By the early hours of the following morning, Minnie was drunk. In addition to that, she was loud and belligerent to the other customers, which prompted the bartender to contact the sheriff. Minnie's disposition had not changed by the time the authorities arrived. She was arrested for intoxication and later released on the condition that she would return to pay a fine. The

Flanked on either side by attractive women, these poker players were certain to return to the gambling dens even if they lost a hand or two. Lady gamblers did more than shuffle cards and deal—they boosted a man's confidence as he played five-card stud, encouraging him to continue laying bets down until he won or was out of money.

moment she was let out of jail, she fled the area and refused to make financial restitution.

Minnie stuck with her plan to set up a sporting house in Creede, and it paid off. Customers flocked to the bordello. She hoped to duplicate her success with a third business in Cripple Creek. Such places were legally restricted there, but Minnie found a way around the situation by calling the bordello a "rooming house."

Competition for business was fierce in the gold mining camp. The other madams operating houses in Cripple Creek and Creede were considerably younger than Minnie and able to attract a regular clientele. By that time, Minnie was forty-five and few took notice of her. In late 1893, after falling into a deep depression, she decided to take her own life. She committed suicide by swallowing a large dose of morphine.

Minnie Smith's body was laid to rest at the Evergreen Cemetery in Colorado Springs. She left a substantial amount of money and property behind, but no one knows what became of her estate.

Jessie Hayman

The San Francisco Favorite

"She had the face and figure of an empress, and the poise and manner of one as well."

THE GRAND DUKE OF RUSSIA'S DESCRIPTION
OF JESSIE HAYMAN, 1908

Jessie Hayman turned the flame down in the gas lamp sitting on a giant fireplace mantle in the parlor of her well-known brothel. Apart from the lit, red lantern hanging off the porch, the room was blanketed in darkness. It was approaching four in the morning, and all of the home's boarders were settled in their rooms with their overnight guests. Madam Hayman's palatial bordello was one of the most popular businesses in San Francisco in 1906. Thirty attractive women of various ages and nationalities worked for Jessie. The income earned from the stable of employees was more than $4,000 a night. Consequently, Jessie was one of the wealthiest madams in the city.

As Jessie went about the routine of closing up shop, a heavy knock on the front door startled her. It was too late for callers but not out of the realm of possibility. As she made her way to the foyer, she removed a pistol from a pocket on her dress. She cocked the gun just as she opened the door and raised it even with the face of a portly man standing opposite her. The stunned man threw his hands up and took a step back. "If you're a gentleman caller who got a late start, please forgive me," Jessie stated firmly. "But if you've come to rob the place, you've got to get past me first."

After apologizing for the intrusion and assuring Jessie that he was merely interested in the company of one of her ladies, the frazzled man stepped inside. Before Jessie had an opportunity to ask about his preferences, he hurried off up the stairs. He seemed to know exactly where he was going. "Guess he's been here before," she said aloud to herself. "Wouldn't do to shoot a regular," she added playfully.

Once she made sure all the doors and windows were locked, she retired to her enormous bedroom. Eight hours later she would open the house again and greet patrons with an enthusiastic smile, a hearty handshake, and a pistol in her pocket. "I keep my customers close and my gun closer," she told friends and family. "It's helped me settle many an argument."

Jessie Hayman was born in 1867 in New Orleans, Louisiana. Her parents, Thad and Constance Wyant, named her Annie May. Very little is known of her childhood. Scholars at the California Historical Library speculate that her family headed west when Annie was a young girl. Her parents died of cholera while en route to the Gold Country, and the orphan eventually turned to prostitution in desperation.

For years she traveled about the various mining camps and cow towns, working as a public woman. Census records indicate that Annie arrived in San Francisco in 1891. By then she was known as Jessie Mellon.

Jessie was the most sought-after boarder of the resorts on Ellis and Post Streets. Nina Hayman was the madam of one of those houses, and she became Jessie's mentor. Nina was kind and patient with her and treated her like a daughter. Jessie was a tall, slender woman with red hair and a bottom men said was "something to watch." She also had a good head for business. Nina encouraged her protégé's talents and promised to help Jessie establish her own house. In 1898 Nina left the trade and married a wealthy lumber dealer. As a parting gift she made good on her promise and turned the brothel over to Jessie. Out of gratitude for her mentor's actions, the thirty-one-year-old Jessie took her madam's last name as her own.

The new Madam Hayman retained the sophisticated air of the three-story home but enhanced the champagne concession in the ballroom. A larger variety of imported, high-priced wines were offered and then served in fine diamond-cut crystal. The much talked-about stemware earned her the nickname "Diamond Jessie."

Jessie's gilded palace was frequented by commoner and royalty alike. A few princes, czars, and dukes from visiting countries paid visits to the resort. In 1899 the Grand Duke of the Imperial Russian Empire spent time with the lovely Madam Hayman and a few of her employees. He was reportedly so enthralled by Jessie's beauty that he invited her to return with him to his homeland. Jessie declined the gracious offer. He then commissioned a life-size painting to be done of her before he left American soil. The twelve to twenty women initially in Jessie's employ thought highly of her. Most paid $5 a day for room and board. Clients were charged $5 to be entertained. Women who were popular, young (fourteen or under), or possessed a special ability charged more for their services and consequently paid more for food and shelter. The average workday hours were from noon to four in the morning. Before the girls retired they bathed in lavender salts and were treated to a massage by the house maids.

The chorus of girls in Jessie's care considered her to be the best madam in the business. She was kind and fair but strict and honest in all her business dealings. One of the house favorites boasted that "Jessie was the tops and when you worked for her you were tops in the business."

Jessie's reputation for being a good madam attracted many girls to her parlor house. She always had more applicants than available positions. Many wanted to work for her because they heard how generous she was to her staff. If more than average amounts of alcohol were consumed during special parties and celebrations, Jessie paid her girls a 5 percent commission from the profits. The girls were allowed to keep any tips they made when they served clients a meal cooked at the house.

Jessie gave a lot to her boarders, and she expected much in return. Her girls were required to act ladylike at all times, to keep themselves clean and neat, and to wear clothing that reflected the high quality of the house. A boarder's wardrobe had to be approved by Jessie before she went to work for her. If her clothing did not fit the ideal the madam had in mind, the boarder had to buy new garments. Jessie advanced her girls money to purchase the gowns needed to entertain. The wardrobe for each girl consisted of a number of expensive items:

1 fox fur for suits: $300

4 tailored suits: $100 each

4 street dresses: $75 each

8 hats for street: $15 each

2 dress coats: $250 each

12 pair street shoes: $18 each

4½ dozen hose: $5 pair

6 pocketbooks: $10 each

2 evening bags: $10 each

½ dozen day gloves: $8 pair

½ dozen evening gloves: $12.50 pair

7 evening gowns: $100 each

7 negligees: $75 each

12 teddy slips: $18 each

24 nightgowns: $20 each

6 pair mules: $15 each

2 evening wraps: $750 each

7 pair evening shoes: $15 each

9 dozen handkerchiefs: $11.50 dozen

6 blouses: $10 each

TOTAL: $6,088.50

In addition to payments for the clothing, deductions were taken from the women's earnings to pay the mistress for maintaining the business and to pay for three full-time maids. A portion of a prostitute's salary also went to pay for doctor's examinations, weekly laundry services, and police payoffs. Jessie was a meticulous bookkeeper and provided her ladies with a weekly account of their finances.

Madam Hayman's attention to detail made her resort the San Francisco favorite. Customers enjoyed the company of the lovely staff and the services that followed the evening. When they arose they found their clothes cleaned and pressed, shoes shined, and an appetizing breakfast awaiting them. Jessie used the money she made from the house and the extras she provided to purchase numerous parcels of land throughout the city.

Enticing photographs were often hung in the parlors of brothels to tempt clients.
AUTHOR'S COLLECTION

On April 18, 1906, Jessie and her boarders were shaken from their beds at five in the morning by a violent earthquake. Her home on Post Street was ruined, but apart from the chimney that had toppled over, the parlor house on Ellis Street suffered little damage. The same could not be said for the majority of the city, however. San Francisco was in ruins, not only from the quakes but also from the subsequent fires. Twenty-eight thousand structures were destroyed over 490 blocks. A quarter of a million people were left homeless, and 450 were dead.

Madam Hayman and many other brothel owners and their employees took it upon themselves to help care for the injured and dying. They helped feed and clothe thousands of homeless who gathered at Golden Gate Park with no other place to go.

Very few parlor houses were left standing after the "great earthquake." Jessie quickly recognized the inherent business opportunity and rebuilt her Post Street house, adding a new wing to her bordello and hiring ten more girls. Neighbors in the area complained to city officials about the late-night activity at Madam Hayman's. The level of tolerance for such an establishment had decreased once the city began the aggressive procedure of rebuilding. Politicians were pressured to crack down on the police who accepted payoffs to overlook prostitution. In the fall of 1905, district attorney William L. Langdon waged war against the brothel patrons and their owners. Langdon was specifically interested in apprehending the wealthiest madam in the business. He issued a warrant for Jessie and put the profession on notice that her arrest was only the beginning.

Jessie was humiliated by the arrest and insulted by the press's claim that she was a "notorious woman in the underworld." After paying the $200 bail, she left the jail and went back to work. She vowed that it would take more than an arrest to give up her business.

A scandal the following year involving a saloon owner, a prominent San Francisco land owner, and Madam Hayman prompted Jessie to close the doors of her Post Street house. When news that the respectable land owner had been frequently seen at Jessie's brothel and was helping to fund the addition to her Post Street house, the pair became the talk of the town. Jessie's partner not only denied their association, but also joined forces with the proprietor of the saloon next door to the bordello and persuaded politicians to shut down the disorderly house.

After the demise of the parlor house on Post Street, Jessie devoted all of her time and attention to her Ellis Street business. Federal laws prohibiting the hiring of prostitutes who had not been in the Unites States more than three years kept her from running the day-to-day operations as she normally did. Many of Jessie's boarders were from France and Russia. Laws were already in place to halt the transportation of such women into the country, but immigration officials felt the code needed to extend to parlor house operators. Jessie was the first madam to be arrested for harboring illegal immigrants.

On August 25, 1908, US marshals raided Jessie's newest home on Mason Street and found an Englishwoman in her hire that had been in the country for only three months. Both she and Jessie were arrested. Jessie's $10,000 bail was raised by several of her friends—prominent men who had spent a great deal of time at her parlor houses.

While awaiting trial on charges of "harboring and maintaining an alien in a house of ill fame," Jessie witnessed the arrest of several other madams in the city. Local police could still be bought off, but federal officials no longer allowed themselves to be manipulated on this matter. Within six months the majority of bordello owners and operators who had spent a fortune on bribing the police and government officials were arrested and carted off to jail.

At the trial Jessie took the stand in her own defense and testified that the young woman working for her was not a prostitute but an entertainer hired to sing and perform on the piano. The federal officers testified differently and submitted proof that the young girl was indeed a prostitute and had worked for several parlor houses throughout the West before settling at Jessie's place. Jessie cried and pleaded with the jury to believe her version of the story, but they were not persuaded. Jessie was found guilty and sentenced to a $300 fine and thirty days in jail. Madam Hayman served her time at a prison in Alameda and then returned to work at yet another house on Mason Street.

After remaining there for a short time, she decided to close the location and open a new business across town. Jessie's grand establishment on Eddy Street was another three-story building with three fireplaces, a saloon, fifteen suites, a dining room, and a massive kitchen. According to boarder Beverly Davis, who lived and worked at the location, the interior was an impressive site:

> *She had a champagne cellar with wine from all parts of the world. Whoever furnished the house knew his stuff. There was a red room, the Turkish room, the French room, the blue room. Oriental couches and shaded lamps, such plush rooms, one after another with deep carpets on the floor. The bedroom upstairs was done in the best style. It reflected the tone of the parlor house all the way through.*

The number of boarders at Madam Hayman's Eddy Street location varied from twelve to fifteen women. In 1912 all of the ladies in her employ were Americans. The list of residents included two girls from Tennessee, one from Kentucky, three from Missouri, two from Colorado, one from Nebraska, four from California, and two sisters who were Comanche Indians from Texas.

After sixteen years as a San Francisco madam, Jessie Hayman retired and decided to travel the world. She toured a variety of countries, including Japan, China, India, Palestine, and Egypt. On March 31, 1923, in a hotel room in London, she died from a massive heart attack. A maid found Jessie seated in a chair. She was elegantly dressed for dinner and wearing many of the diamonds she had acquired over her lifetime. The fifty-six-year-old ex-madam never married. She left the bulk of her $116,000 estate to her eight-year-old niece, her five brothers and sisters, and her two cats.

Gertrudis Maria Barceló

The Evening Angel

"A female was dealing and had you looked in her countenance for any symptom by which to discover how the game stood, you would have turned away unsatisfied; for calm seriousness was alone discernable and the cards fell from her fingers as steadily as though she was handling only a knitting needle."

TRAVELING ACTOR MATT FIELD, 1839

A smartly dressed man stopped just outside the Barceló Palace in Santa Fe, New Mexico, and flicked a speck of alkali dust from the black satin lapel of his immaculate frock coat. He then inspected the creases in the legs of his trousers and gave his expensive brocade waistcoat a firm tug. It didn't do for people to enter one of the finest gambling houses in the West in disarray. Cardsharps and faro dealers at the Palace could always spot an amateur gambler by the way he dressed. Any professional would know that proper attire in such an establishment was a must. Gertrudis Maria Barceló, the alluring owner of the gambling house, expected the clientele to reflect the sophisticated atmosphere of the business itself.

The charming, cigar-smoking lady gambler first began welcoming guests into her lavish business in 1842. After shaking the dust and mud from the street off their boots, patrons stepped onto a plush carpet that led to a massive mahogany bar. The gigantic room, which housed a number of stylish accoutrements, featured ornate mirrors on every wall. Spectacular chandeliers hung from the ceiling, and exotic statues from Europe added to the posh setting.

Upon entering the Barceló Palace, wealthy gamblers were escorted by handsome women in Maria's employ to private card rooms. There, the sultry proprietor dealt cards for a poker game called monte. The popular game was easy and fast. Any number of people could play against the dealer, also known as the bank. The game worked this way: The bank drew one card from the bottom of the deck and placed it faceup on the table. This was known as the bottom layout. One card was then drawn from the top of the pack and placed faceup on the table for the top layout. The players (also called punters) bet on either layout. The pack was then turned faceup, and the card showing on the bottom was known as the gate. If the suit of this card (heart, spade, etc.) matched one of the layouts, the banker paid the bet. The banker won the bet if the gate was not the same suit as the layout.

Maria was known as the Queen of the Monte Dealers. She was a shrewd banker with agile fingers and a poker face that very few could ever read. In between hands she kept her affluent clientele comfortable, serving them free alcohol and providing them with a lavish array of food to eat. An assortment of delicious pastries, cheeses, and meats was offered around the clock. And when the men were through at the tables, the entertainment continued upstairs with the sporting women who had led them to Maria at the start of their visit.

Señora Barceló, or La Tules, as she would later be called (translated, the name means Gertrude), was born in Sonora, Mexico, in 1800. Her parents were extremely wealthy and lavished their daughter with every advantage, including an education. Maria was bright, ambitious, fiercely independent, and stunning. She had a dark complexion, long black hair, and dark eyes. From an early age she possessed the self-assurance of a person who knew how to take care of herself.

In 1823 she demonstrated her autonomy by going against her father's wishes and marrying a man of very little means named Jose Cisneros y Lucero. In an effort to assert her own self-reliance and prove that the gentleman married her for love and not money, Maria insisted he sign a prenuptial agreement of sorts. The agreement allowed her to retain her maiden name, the money and property she was destined to inherit, and the right to enter into business negotiations on her own. The deal she struck was unconventional but proved to be a wise move.

Before Maria and her husband settled in Santa Fe, the couple visited the saloons and dance halls in Albuquerque and Taos to gamble. The pair enjoyed playing poker and sat in on a variety of games, with Maria always winning more than she lost.

Gertrudis Maria Barceló was a charming, cigar-smoking poker player known as the Queen of the Monte Dealers. Her gaming house in Santa Fe was a posh establishment with wall-to-wall mirrors.
LIBRARY OF CONGRESS, LC-DIG-PPMSCA-02901

Using her substantial earnings and a portion of her dowry, Maria set up her own gambling parlor near a rich mining camp in the Ortiz Mountains. With her spouse by her side, the two operated the casino, making fast enemies of the intoxicated prospectors who lost to them and believed they were cheats. The pair was redeemed in the eyes of their patrons after they managed to separate two of the area's most respected and best poker players from a large amount of cash.

Maria dreamed of more than running a low-rent, high-stakes gaming den frequented by unrefined men. She wanted an opulent parlor that would attract patrons. In 1826 she purchased a grand saloon and filled it with expensive furniture and velvet curtains. The Barceló Palace quickly became a favorite with Santa Fe's fashionable society.

Most nights the gambling house was occupied solely with monte players and five-card draw enthusiasts, but on special occasions Maria reserved the facility for fancy balls. The elaborate parties were attended by Mexican officers from a nearby post. She hosted such celebrations to commend the military leaders for their service and entice potential gamblers.

The Palace was well known throughout the New Mexico area, not only for its high-class games but also for the female staff that worked there. Maria's women were fashionable, impeccably groomed ladies who serviced the various gamblers in their rooms on the top floor of the establishment. The "evening angels," as they were called, were provided with fine, spangled dresses, jewelry, and hand-tooled belts complete with a hidden derringer. If any customer got out of line, the girls were instructed to defend themselves.

In addition to being a successful business owner, Madam Barceló was a calculating investor. She increased her wealth by bankrolling mining ventures, hotels, and freight lines. She operated her empire from behind a green felt monte table. Thousands of dollars passed through her hands as well as valuable information about the Mexican government's intention to overtake the American civilian government office in Santa Fe.

The war between Mexico and the United States began with a struggle over who would control Texas and extended over the entire Southwest. Maria came down on the side of the United States. She supported its efforts by loaning troops money and providing them with necessary supplies. After learning of an eminent attack against the government by the Mexican Indians, she alerted the American authorities. The scheme, which was scheduled to take place in December 1846, was subsequently thwarted.

Maria's husband did not approve of her involvement with the Anglo army, but that was just one of many areas in which he did not share her views. His wife kept company with many leading politicians, and it was rumored that her relationships went well beyond discussing the emerging United States boundaries. Among the many affairs historians note that

La Tules had was one with the governor of New Mexico, General Manuel Armijo. Jose eventually tired of his wife's philandering, and the two went their separate ways in 1848, a few months after the United States and Mexico signed the Treaty of Guadalupe Hidalgo.

Senora Barceló's marriage may not have lasted a lifetime, but her time at the monte table did. Maria lived out the remainder of her life managing her famous gambling hall and dealing cards. One visitor who stopped by the Palace in 1850 recorded in his journal that "the fine lady La Tules had become wealthy dealing monte . . . and even at the age of 50 was lovely and her bank was almost always open."

When Maria Barceló passed away in January 1852, she was the richest woman in Santa Fe. Her funeral was just as extravagant as the gambling parlor she called home. The Catholic church that hosted her burial service was lit with hundreds of candles. Several men dressed in handsome vaquero costumes and high-peaked sombreros trimmed with metal conchos were in attendance. She was remembered by those present as "sylphlike in movement with a slender figure and a finely featured face . . . a beautiful woman with a steady proud head and the demeanor of a wild cat."

The fortune she left behind included several houses, livestock, and cash. It was divided among her family members, the church, and city officials to be used for charitable work.

Josie Washburn

Nebraska's Reluctant Madam

"From reckless despair she drifted into the life; it is with determination bordering on recklessness that she starts to quit it."
JOSIE WASHBURN'S THOUGHTS ON THE
REFORMATION OF A PROSTITUTE, 1905

A large wagon filled with fallen angels rattled down a dusty street in Lincoln, Nebraska. It was daylight, but a hard rain obscured the sun. Three armed sheriff's deputies walked alongside the crowded vehicle, grinning from ear to ear. Raindrops bounced off the tin badges pinned to their slickers. The drenched passengers huddled together like chickens caught in a storm.

Dignified citizens stared out of shop windows and saloon doors at the public women under arrest that were being paraded through town. Some of the humiliated prostitutes hid their faces with scarves; others hung their heads in shame. Josie Washburn, a pretty, neatly dressed brunette in the center of the wagon, kept her eyes fixed on the gawking residents. Her pride was wounded, but she refused to give them the satisfaction of seeing that she'd been broken.

The ride to the jail was slow and deliberate. Lightening streaked across the sky, and the rain fell in sheets. As the wagon passed by the bank, two businessmen stepped into the doorframe and laughed at the sight of the soaked women. The insensitive chortles brought the maniacal rage lapping at Josie's senses to a high flame. At once she was on her feet. "You don't think we have feelings!" she shouted. "We may be whores, but we have feelings just like anyone else."

Thunder rolled overhead. Josie glanced around at the stunned onlookers. "You need us to protect the good women here, you say!" She bellowed over the sound of the violent weather. "And you treat us like livestock!"

One of the deputies ordered her to "sit down and shut up." Josie glared at him. He leveled his shotgun at her and pumped the barrel. "Go ahead," she dared him. "Put me out of their misery."

Until Josie Washburn was motivated to do so, almost no one spoke out on behalf of public women. They were talked about, mistreated, and shunned by society, but little understanding was given to why some women were driven to prostitution. Josie's lone voice and extensive writing on the subject exposed the conditions that perpetuated the profession.

Josie began working at parlor houses in Omaha, Nebraska, in August 1871. She was seventeen years old. Born in the Northeast to parents of Scottish and Norwegian decent, she was given the name Helena. Anna Wilson, the first madam the young girl worked for, changed Helena's name to one that was more suitable for the trade. Historians speculate that Josie was abandoned at an early age and forced to make her own way. Job opportunities for women were limited. Desperation and the threat of starvation led many to the profession.

Anna's brothel was a home for Josie and the other girls who worked there. For many of them it was the first place they felt they belonged. In spite of the dire circumstances, a sense of family prevailed among the residents of the house. Josie stayed at Anna's for more than eight years.

Josie was arrested numerous times on prostitution charges during her employment at Madam Wilson's. The public humiliation of being dragged into court took its toll on her after time. The shame she felt for the life she was forced to live overshadowed the devotion she had for Anna and the other women at the house. Unable to continue on, Josie attempted to kill herself using a borrowed revolver. Her unsteady hand caused the weapon to miss its intended mark. She suffered a bullet wound, but it was not fatal. Newspaper reports claimed the shooting was an accident.

A proposal of marriage gave Josie the chance to escape her sad lifestyle. When she exchanged vows with Frank Stone in early 1880, she believed her future had great promise. Stone was an educated man, and Josie was deeply in love with him. For fifteen years the pair drifted from one western town to the next. Frank proved to be anything but reliable.

Posting a photograph alongside a prostitute's license was an effective advertising ploy.
AUTHOR'S COLLECTION

He was bad with money and gambled away large sums. He frequently left his wife alone for months at a time. Josie was devastated by his actions and in 1907 wrote about her disappointment:

A man expects his wife to be an angel under any and all circumstances. The man pledges his protection, care and love for life, and upon these terms the woman becomes his wife, in full confidence that this love is permanent and lasting; in sickness or health she has a right to expect him to be true to her.

The great burden of married life comes to the wife, who has her household duties, and the children to care for, and a thousand and one things to perform which make up the daily routine.

When the husband comes home from his daily occupation, his wife has a right to expect his company during the evening; to her his presence is company, even though he chooses to bury himself in his newspapers.

But she does not receive this consideration. He is absent night after night and often until the break of day, or for several days. When he arrives he is nervous and grouchy, and throws things around. While he is changing his wearing apparel he loses the proverbial collar buttons, strewing them upon the floor, and cussing because they are not as large as sledge-hammers. A man in that condition isn't noted for his nimble fingers among other deficiencies. His wife comes to his rescue, fastens his collar, and observes that his breath hasn't the aroma of violets, nor his blood-shot eyes the expression of remorse; he does not make the effort to hold his temper that he did the collar-button. With a scowl he tells his wife that he has been at a banquet.

He remains at home for a night or two to rest up. Then he goes to another banquet, or club or he is called away from town on a matter of business, or important transactions kept him at the office, or he met some friends at a hotel who detained him; he volunteers this information without any interrogations from his wife, who trembles with fear that something is wrong. When men go out in bunches, they sometimes frankly admit to their wives that they have been out with the boys seeing the sights, but they don't tell what they saw.

In 1895 Frank abandoned Josie for good. He left her with numerous debts and no viable income. She was forced to return to the type of work she often referred to as the "underworld sewer." Josie settled in Lincoln, Nebraska, and, after earning a substantial amount of money working as a prostitute, opened her own parlor house. Historical records show that she had five employees in June 1900. The clients that frequented her business were from all walks of life: politicians and pioneers, preachers and police.

Josie took her job as madam seriously, looking out for the ladies in her hire in much the same way Anna Wilson had looked after her. According to Josie's memoirs, "A wise matron of the underworld is a woman of many resources and sound judgment, which is gained by experience so severe that you would not believe it possible for a human being to endure." Josie treated her staff with kindness and respect and protected them from violent men, drug sellers, thieves, and gamblers. "The madam is the best friend a girl has," Josie wrote in her autobiography. Josie did her best to look out for her boarders' well-being, but she could not protect them from the "violations" she was sure they would encounter once the bedroom door closed behind them. She believed that prostitutes "lost a bit of their soul each time they entertained a client." Women new to the profession harbored the misconception that the wealthier a client was, the better they would be treated. Josie made it clear that the opposite was true.

> *Upon the first arrival of the girl, she imagines that all her troubles will be gone when she becomes acquainted with the rich man, but there is no class of men who are less generous than the rich man when he is sober, although he will spend thousands of dollars for self-indulgence, buying champagne by the case. He will order all that the bunch can drink, waste, lave and wallow in.*
>
> *The girls are required to take a part in the lowest debauchery, for the amusement of this man, for which they are liberally supplied with money, besides the madam's rake-off isn't small; through all kinds of confusion she never loses sight of the business at hand.*
>
> *After a girl has been through one of these orgies with the rich man, there is nothing left in the line of vice that is not familiar to her. A girl might be in some parts of the underworld for years, and not have the knowledge or experience in vice that these girls have learned under the direction of one rich man, in a week or a month's extreme revelry.*

Prostitution in Nebraska in the early 1900s was a lucrative line of work, and Josie Washburn's house made a great deal of money. She and her girls were required to pay large sums to public officials to stay in operation, however. As the madam, Josie was required to pay a monthly protection fee of $14.70 to $29.70. Law enforcement officers varied in the way they collected the payments. Some were satisfied with allowing Josie to submit the payment through a messenger. Others required individual prostitutes to pay the fee in person at the jail. Women who did not have the money owed were thrown into a cell and held there until their bill was paid.

"We always went [to the jail] with fear and trembling," wrote Josie. "Whenever law enforcement wanted to prove to the public at large that prostitution was not being tolerated, they would load women from various parlor houses into a mud wagon and parade them through town. We regarded this treatment as unjust and cruel, but the effect was to make us more willing to part with our cash."

The experience of being "held up" by officers of the law happened repeatedly in the underworld.

Opportunities for employment for men were vast. They could take any career path they wanted. Frontier women did not have the same advantages. So when men chose to own and operate a brothel, Josie was highly resentful. She considered "male-landladies" or "P.I.s" (an abbreviation for pimp) to be the most despicable members of the underworld.

There is one (P.I.) in the city of Omaha who owns the greater share of the red-light district, which is of no small proportions in this city.

This he-landlady leases and controls several alleys, on which he has built rows of cribs, both sides similarly arranged. Each crib consists of two small rooms, about six feet high; a door and a window forms the whole front. Each crib has a projecting corner, and a casual glance down the line gives it a scalloped appearance, which is meant to be artistic. . . .

Some of the girls who exist in these alleys are those who have seen years of suffering, and are now addicted to dope and liquor. But the majority are the very young girls who are carried away by the excitement. . . .

From these cribs, and the many big houses, is the deriving source of the monster's great wealth—he who has paid the police and influenced politicians in his behalf for years. His monthly income from this horrible traffic is several thousands of dollars. He has become very wealthy from the pitiful earnings of human beings in debauchery.

Whether spent as a prostitute or a madam, Josie's years in the trade were filled with degradation and deception. "If one is to be successful financially, they must assume a variety of distasteful roles, lover, confidant and entertainer," Josie admitted. Big-money customers were made to feel like they were the house's favorite clients. In truth they considered these men to be worthless.

"We haven't any regard for him in our hearts, knowing that he has left a loving and truthful wife at home, who is counting the minutes of his absence," she wrote.

Public women were considered outcasts by churches, and hospitals turned them away when they came searching for health care. "Our women have absolutely no friends outside of their world," Josie lamented in her journals. "No flood of pity will rush into the souls of good people for our belief." She was appalled that laws were in place to prohibit the abuse of dogs, but there were no laws at all to protect and care for sporting women.

Josie retired in 1907 and found legitimate work managing a boardinghouse. Hoping to educate people about the misery associated with the life of a public woman and the exploitation of prostitutes by ruthless businessmen and government officials, Josie began writing a book. Using the journal entries and notes she had penned over her twenty-one years in the business, she created a manuscript that described the horrible condition inherent with the social evil. She blamed corrupt men for the continuation of prostitution and noted that no matter what they might say, opponents would never abolish the profession. "As long as men desire the services found at parlor houses," she wrote, "there will be men who solicit women for such services. Too many men derive wealth and political influence from prostitution to willingly end it."

Josie's attempt to bring about change in the trade went beyond authoring a book. In 1911 she asked the Nebraska legislature for funds to build a home for prostitutes who wanted to leave the business. Her request of $100,000 was denied. She countered:

That the underworld woman is not permitted to reform is the firm conviction of all of our people.

This conclusion is forced upon us by the decision of the Christian world, which is that if a woman has fallen she will never reform, and there is no use to try to help her.

If the men, young or old, who come to us in our castles, houses, cribs, or dives, and associate with us in the sin of the underworld, should be disgraced and branded by the Christian and business world, this would go a long way toward reformation, as the men would try to avoid the disgrace.

Does the Christian man or woman refuse to associate on equal terms with a man who is our associate and supplies the money which keeps your institutions going?

Not long after Josie was denied the capital for her project, she relocated to Minneapolis and concentrated her efforts on getting her book published. The subject matter of her book made it impossible for her to find a publisher. The male-dominated industry took offense at her claim that the root of prostitution could be traced to men.

Rejection from mainstream publishers only made Josie more determined to see her work in print. In 1925 she invested her own money and published the book, *The Underworld Sewer*, herself. She dedicated the work to the people of "Village, City, State and Nation, which both consciously and unconsciously maintain the social evil."

Three years after the book was released Josie moved to Spokane, Washington. All traces of her then disappeared. Historians speculate that she changed her name and started a new life, putting to rest her tainted, pitiful past forever.

Kate O'Leary

The Redheaded Rival

"Rowdy Kate was a fine limbed powerful woman who was the only one who could handle the cowboys when they got too much of the cordials served at the bar."

CIRCUS OWNER COLONEL LEWIS GINGER, 1870

A hard rain was falling outside a modest cabin situated in the center of a barren stretch of land outside Kansas City, Kansas. Magnificent claps of thunder shook the structure, and bolts of lightning lit up the night sky and danced across the empty prairie valley. Kate O'Leary lay in bed, unable to sleep, staring out the window at the storm. In the near distance she could hear the sound of fast-approaching horses' hooves. She quickly sat up and leaned back on the crude wooden headboard, waiting. A knock on the door a few moments later brought her to her feet. "Who is it?" she demanded through the unopened door. "We're here with your husband, ma'am," a voice responded.

Kate cinched her robe tightly closed and swung the heavy wooden frame open. Three rain-soaked riders wearing dour expressions greeted the woman. "Where's Bill?" Kate asked after scanning the faces of the strangers. One of the men stepped down off his horse and, trudging through the mud, made his way to the ride behind him. A body wrapped in several drenched blankets was lying across the saddle.

Kate's eyes filled with tears as she stood frozen, staring at the bundle. A gust of wind blew the relentless rain across her petite frame and distraught face. "He made us promise to bring him home, ma'am," one of the riders said sympathetically. Kate slowly approached the lifeless form, reached out her hands, and rolled the blankets off the bruised, blue face hidden under them. Deep rope burns around the dead man's neck bore witness as to how he had arrived at the unfortunate state.

Rowdy Katie O'Leary entertained many cowboys, trappers, and prospectors as she dealt hands of poker to the enchanted men who were willing to lose their money to her. She used her winnings to purchase a gambling den of her own in Dodge City, Kansas.
SEARLS HISTORICAL LIBRARY

"You are Kate O'Leary, ain't ya?" the third man inquired. Kate simply nodded. "What did he do?" she asked. The rider explained that Bill was a cattle rustler and horse thief who had eluded the authorities for some time. After the outlaw and two of his cohorts were apprehended in the act of stealing, the men admitted to their crimes. "You hang people without a trial?" Kate snapped. Thunder rolled overhead as the men revealed that they were members of the Anti–Horse Thief Association and duty bound to deal harshly with such criminals.

The vigilantes handed the sorrowful widow a leather pouch containing $400 and told Kate it was all that was on Bill at the time of his demise. They lifted the thief's body off the horse and gently laid him on the ground outside the cabin door. They politely tipped their hats to the forlorn Kate and rode away into the stormy night.

The following day Kate O'Leary buried her husband in the town cemetery. She stood over the freshly covered grave, shaking with great sobs. After several hours friends led the grieving widow away from the burial plot and back to her home, where she was left alone to contemplate her future.

Career options for single women on the Kansas plains in 1869 were limited. But Kate was determined to do what was available to get by. She was a quick-witted, stunning beauty with an hourglass figure and long, red-gold hair, attributes that were well received by saloon patrons everywhere. Kate decided her job opportunities would be better in a bigger town, so she packed her meager belongings and headed to Dodge City.

She was an instant success with the cowhands and trail busters who frequented the taverns in the wild burg. When Kate entered a dance hall, she stood out like a flame.

It wasn't the life her family had imagined for their child when she was a little girl growing up on a farm situated on the border of Missouri and Kansas. The grandmother who raised her had been a schoolteacher, and at one time Kate had considered entering the field. The exposure she had to the rough characters who passed through the area where she lived left a lasting impression on Kate and changed her outlook on the profession. Compared to the lifestyle of the fast-talking gamblers and ever-moving ranch hands, teaching was a bit too tame.

Kate's grandmother tried to bring the restless girl's thoughts back to more appropriate pursuits. She even sent the teenager to a girls' school in Kansas City, but it was to no avail. By the time she was fourteen years old, Kate had abandoned all thought of becoming a teacher.

When typhoid fever claimed the lives of her grandmother and father, Kate was forced to find work to support herself. She hired on as a waitress in a hotel in Dodge City that catered to cattlemen. Her charming personality and good looks made her a favorite with the patrons. Bill O'Leary was one of the enamored customers. Bill and Kate hadn't been courting long before he proposed. They were married a month after their first meeting.

Bill was kind but mysterious. He always carried large amounts of cash, and whenever he left for work he would be gone for days. He never shared his whereabouts with Kate and remained tight-lipped when asked about his job. He provided her with all the comforts she could imagine: clothing, jewelry, thoroughbred horses, and a new ranch house. Kate never suspected Bill was involved in anything illegal, and she overlooked his curious behavior when he would finally arrive home and shower her with gifts. It wasn't until her husband was escorted home by three members of the Anti–Horse Thief Association that she fully accepted his occupation was that of a crook.

Kate used a portion of the money Bill left her to purchase a dance hall and bordello. Thirsty patrons at Kate's establishment were treated to the finest whiskey in the area and the company of one of six prostitutes. They were also invited to join the proprietor at the gaming table for a hand of poker. Kate had learned the game as a child and perfected her skills playing against her late husband. She dealt cards nightly, raking in a sizable amount in the process.

Kate's place was one of Dodge City's most popular watering holes. Customers traveled back and forth from her business to another well-known saloon across town that was run by Joseph Lowe. Lowe was handsome, ambitious, and an immaculate dresser. He was a gambler, too, with a strong attraction for his redheaded rival. Kate couldn't resist his charms, and in late 1870 the pair began a romantic relationship.

The coupling was a volatile and passionate one. Nineteen-year-old Kate and twenty-year-old Joe fought constantly, each refusing to alter their immoral lifestyle for the other. Both had quick tempers and were prone to jealousy, and more than once tried to outplay each other at poker. In spite of their dueling personalities, however, they were committed to one another and very much in love.

In 1871 Kate and Joe sold their individual businesses and moved to Newton, Kansas. Upon arriving in the busy cow town, they jointly purchased a combination saloon / gambling den / brothel. The lovers' "house of ill fame" was the hub of activity, and townspeople referred to the impetuous owners as Rowdy Kate and Rowdy Joe.

Law enforcement paid frequent visits to the Rowdys' place. Sometimes they were just customers, but oftentimes they were there to keep the peace. Joe had a talent with a six-shooter and was not opposed to drawing on someone trying to cheat at cards or flirt with Kate. When a traveling gunman persuaded Rowdy Kate to sneak off with him on February 19, 1872, Rowdy Joe went after them. He caught the pair at a competing brothel and shot the man in the chest. The controversy surrounding the man's death forced Joe and Kate to relocate.

After leaving Newton the couple settled in Wichita. They bought another saloon and went back to work gambling and selling drinks and female companionship. It didn't take long for trouble to catch up with them again. Kate was a beautiful woman and attracted a lot of attention. Overt advances made by the clientele enraged Joe and brought on a violent response. His reputation as a hard man and a tough opponent in a fight grew. He pistol-whipped one customer and bit the ear off another for getting drunk and making a pass at Kate.

Together Rowdy Joe and Rowdy Kate were involved in a dispute with a competing saloon owner named E. T. "Red" Beard. They fought over customers, employees, and drink prices. Beard's temperament matched Joe's, and he wasn't opposed to settling disagreements with his fists or a gun. On October 27, 1883, Beard used both methods to handle a problem with a soiled dove named Josephine DeMerritt. The argument between the two started at Beard's saloon but quickly shifted to Kate and Joe's gambling den.

Beard was drunk when he chased his lover out of his place and into the Rowdys' establishment, located a mere fifty feet away. Kate was busy dealing cards and Joe was conversing with a half dozen cowhands from Texas when Josephine and Beard burst into the den. Josephine hurried away from the angry man, disappearing down a long corridor of the upstairs bordello. Lifting his gun out of his holster, Beard raced after her. Kate and Joe left their work and quickly hurried after the pair. Each had a weapon drawn. By the time they made it up the stairs, Beard had already fired off a shot. The woman he hit was not Josephine, however. It was Annie Franklin, a prostitute mistaken for the fleeing woman. Joe followed closely after Beard, and Kate remained behind to care for the injured woman.

After a classic street gunfight in which an innocent bystander was caught in the crossfire and blinded, Joe shot Beard in the side. Beard never recovered from the wound. Joe was arrested for the murder, subsequently tried, and acquitted. The man that was left blind from the ordeal pursued a lawsuit against Joe, and he was bound over by the local sheriff's office for another trial. Convinced Joe would not be as lucky in a second hearing, Kate helped her paramour escape custody. She was then arrested for aiding an accused criminal.

Kate was not convicted and was later released. She never saw Rowdy Joe again. He was shot and killed at the Walrus Saloon in Denver on February 11, 1899.

In spite of the demise of her relationship with Joe Lowe and her recent run-ins with the law, Rowdy Kate managed to keep the saloon open for a while. In 1877 she pulled up stakes and moved to Fort Worth, Texas. She purchased another business that catered to the debaucheries of mankind and in no time was turning a hefty profit.

Politicians and citizens opposed to the combination gambling den/saloon/bordello fought such places. On two separate occasions Kate was charged with "keeping a house of ill-fame" and fined $100. The amount was a pittance in comparison to the money she made from the business as a whole.

Kate remained in the Fort Worth area for eleven years. According to records at the Kansas Historical Society, she then moved on to Big Springs, a fast-growing cattle town in the heart of Texas. From there she went to Fort Griffin and continued with her usual line of work, gambling and managing prostitutes.

In 1888 Kate was traveling via stage from Fort Griffin to Fort Worth and back again when she met a little girl who changed the course of her life. The stage passed the young girl afoot on the road, and she ran after the vehicle, begging the driver to stop. When he did she asked if the road she was on led to Fort Griffin. The driver assured her it did and then hurried his team along. Kate witnessed the exchange, took pity on the child, and demanded the driver stop to give her a ride. At first the teamster refused, stating he believed the girl had no money for a ticket. After Kate paid for the girl's passage, the stage stopped.

Once aboard, the girl told Kate that she was an orphan and had no home. Upon their arrival in Fort Griffin, Kate made arrangements for the local hotel owner and his wife to take the child into their home. The couple, who had one adopted son, eventually adopted the girl. The child grew up to be a schoolteacher, and she and Kate were a major part of one another's lives.

According to Josiah Wright Mooar, a buffalo hunter and one of Kate's closest friends, the close relationship she had with the girl helped change her immoral ways. Kate was a surrogate aunt and took her responsibility for the child seriously. The reformation included giving up operating saloons and bordellos and playing cards. She attended church regularly and raised funds for various charitable endeavors. Rowdy Kate died in 1928 in San Angelo, Texas. She was estimated to have been seventy-three years old.

Martha Jane Canary

The Black Hills Calamity

"I was considered the most reckless and daring rider and one of the best shots in the western country."

Calamity Jane, 1896

A massive wagon train, 190 people strong, inched its way into the booming metropolis of Deadwood, South Dakota. The dusty, white canvas tops of the slow-moving vehicles could be seen for miles by anyone who might have glanced into the near distance. Most residents weren't that interested in newcomers to the congested gold rush camp. Business owners along the main thoroughfare might have felt differently, but many viewed the presence of more settlers as competition for the gold in the Black Hills.

The procession of Conestoga wagons would hardly have been noticed if not for the two figures escorting the caravan. The normally preoccupied citizens who caught a glimpse of the buckskin-clad riders took time out of their usual routine of prospecting, purchasing supplies, and visiting various saloons to watch the train lumber along. Richard Hughes, a reporter for the *Black Hills Daily Times,* was the first to recognize the outriders as Wild Bill Hickok and Calamity Jane.

"The two were dressed in buckskin with sufficient fringe to make a buckskin rope," Hughes later wrote. "They were both wearing white Stetsons and clean boots. Jane was an Amazonian woman of the frontier, clad in complete male habiliments and riding astride. Yelling and whooping, she waved her fancy Stetson at all the men jammed into the crooked, narrow street."

Calamity Jane's entrance into Deadwood Gulch in June 1876 was an appropriate beginning for the eventful life she would lead during her time there. In addition to her nonconforming manner of dress, she was exceptionally skilled in areas traditionally reserved for men. She drove heavy freight wagons over rough western terrain, cracking a bullwhip with expert precision. She could ride, rope, drink, curse, and gamble with the best of the male population and if provoked would even fistfight with the opposite sex.

If curious miners missed the commotion surrounding her first arrival into the area, they need not have been disappointed; another public display would not be far behind.

Calamity Jane began acting out against what the world thought a girl should be like when she was a youngster. Ornery cousins who pelted her with corncobs in hopes that their action would make her cry were surprised when she stood up to them, hurling expletives their way.

She was born in Princeton, Missouri, on May 1, 1852. Her mother, Charlotte Canary, named her Martha Jane. According to historian Duncan Aikman, Calamity came by her unconventional attitude honestly. Charlotte was an original thinker as well. She wore bold colored dresses many considered gaudy and flirted openly with men who could not resist her striking good looks. Her husband, Robert Canary, tried desperately to reform his wife and keep the town from talking about her shameless behavior, but was unable to do so.

Robert spent long hours farming in the fields around the family home. Charlotte busied herself doing anything other than making sure her children were close by. Calamity and her siblings were generally left to their own devices. Calamity spent the bulk of her time with neighboring boys, riding horses, hunting, and swimming in the watering hole. Calamity was more comfortable around rowdy boys than properly behaved little girls. In her estimation boys seemed to have more fun and weren't afraid of getting a little dirty. By the time Robert decided to move his wife and children west of the Mississippi, Calamity was a twelve-year-old rebel. A tomboy who snuck drinks of whiskey and the occasional chew of tobacco, she preferred pants to dresses and riding to cooking.

Calamity's wild, unconventional ways fit right in with the untamed frontier. As the Canarys made their way west, Calamity roamed the countryside on horseback. When she wasn't exploring the new land she was learning how to be a teamster. She practiced with the same thirty-foot bullwhip the wagon train leader used to get the livestock to hurry along.

Calamity Jane was a true western legend. She lived an unconventional life for a woman of her time.

The bullwhackers taught the young girl much more than how to snap a whip. Her education included how to smoke a cigar, play poker, and swear. The latter was a trait she would eventually elevate to an art form. In years to come she would be named the "champion swearer of the Black Hills of Dakota."

Calamity continued to feel more at ease with men than women as she grew older. In her autobiography she noted that men "were as rough and unpredictable as the wild country she had fallen in love with." While other preteen girls dreamed of motherhood, social status, or a career on stage, Jane wanted only to pursue her exploration of the high prairie.

The rowdy life surrounding the mining community of Virginia City, New Mexico, where the Canarys settled, suited Calamity. She liked the sounds emanating from the saloons and the gunfights that played out up and down the streets. Her parents were so engrossed in themselves and their own problems, both marital and financial, that they paid little or no attention to where Calamity and her brothers and sister were spending their time. In fact, days would pass when neither Charlotte nor Robert would be home at all. The Canary children were forced to fend for themselves.

In 1865 Calamity's father passed away, and a year later her mother died. Robert's death is believed to have been a suicide and Charlotte was stricken with pneumonia. At fifteen years of age, Jane took over the care of her siblings. It wasn't long before the task proved to be too overwhelming and she abandoned the responsibility and headed to Salt Lake City, Utah.

The bawdy community was crowded with soldiers from nearby military posts Fort Steele and Fort Bridger. Calamity made several of the men's acquaintance, picking their brains about their experiences in the service, sharing a drink or two with them, and joining in on a game of poker. She wasn't the best card player, but occasionally she got lucky enough to win a hand. Her winnings kept her in food, alcohol, and cigars.

At sixteen Calamity took a job as a bullwhacker for a wagon train of hunters. News of a woman working in such a capacity spread from town to town. People referred to her as that "Canary girl—the one that drinks a quart of whiskey and curses like your grandfather and can drive a team like mad."

Over the next eight years, Calamity would be employed by a variety of wagon freight lines throughout the West. In the process she became thoroughly acquainted with the terrain and its native inhabitants. As time went on and her reputation as a tough woman teamster grew, she boldly began to challenge saloon owners' policies about serving females. In Cheyenne, Wyoming, she marched into a tavern on Main Street and ordered herself a drink. It was the first of many saloons where she would enjoy a libation. With only one exception, she was always served promptly. When a bartender in Denver, Colorado, refused to provide her with a shot, she pushed the barrel of her pistol into his face and demanded he rethink his position.

Calamity was not content with only being allowed to drink in saloons; she wanted to be able to gamble publicly as well. She particularly enjoyed a hand of five-card stud. Seldom if ever did she spend any time at the faro tables. She believed that "chance always favored the house" in that game.

It was while drinking and playing cards that Calamity found the best audience for her many tales. They served to further enhance her already inflated reputation with the westward pioneers. In early 1877, while gambling at a Rapid City saloon, an inebriated Jane told the men in the game with her about her time scouting for General George Custer. The cowhands turned their attention away from their cards and focused solely on Calamity. Custer had met his end in July the previous year at the Battle of the Little Bighorn, and interest in his Seventh Cavalry troops and in the boy general himself was high. In her autobiography she told the story this way:

"In the spring of 1876, we were ordered north with General Crook to join General Miles, Terry and Custer at Big Horn River. During this march I swam the Platte River at Fort Fetterman as I was the bearer of important dispatches. I had a 90 mile ride to make, being wet and cold, I contracted a severe illness and was sent back in General Crook's ambulance to Fort Fetterman where I laid in the hospital for 14 days."

Historians doubt her story to be entirely true. In an article that appeared in the *Sioux Falls Argus-Leader* in 1906, writer George Hoshier, who knew Calamity, scoffed at her claim. "She did come into the hills with General Crook and wore men's clothing at that time, but she was no more a scout than I was."

True or not, Calamity's story achieved the desired twofold effect. The more she talked, the more drinks the men she was playing poker with bought her. Their concentration on the cards was shaken to the point that they lost the majority of hands to the legendary character.

Calamity Jane's adventures as a stage driver, bullwhacker, and part-time nurse were captured in several dime novels. Released in the 1870s, the publications further blurred the line between truth and fabrication. They did, however, make for good reading and transform the rugged woman, who had actually known a string of jobs from laundress to prostitution, into a celebrity. The notoriety prompted gamblers across the West to invite Jane to sit in on a hand and was worth countless rounds of drinks.

Calamity acquired her handle in the early 1870s, and there are almost as many explanations as to how she got the name as there are old-timers. Among the most popular explanations is the one from Aikman, who writes that "Calamity was associated with her because she carried guns ostentatiously, suffered through several buggy accidents and was generally considered unlucky." Other historians note that the name was given to her by an army lieutenant she nursed back to health after he had suffered through a bout with smallpox. He called her "an angel in calamity."

After getting to know James Butler Hickok in 1872 through her friend Buffalo Bill Cody, Jane hoped her days of being in the center of one adversity after another had finally ended. Since she and the dashing lawman/gunfighter had first met, she had been taken with him. Hickok was fascinated with Calamity's bravado and amused by her wild antics. The pair was destined to become friends. She wanted there to be more, but Hickok was not interested in her in that way. When she rode into Deadwood with him in 1876, she had a fleeting hope that he might change his mind about her.

Calamity Jane followed Wild Bill in and out of the gambling dens like a smitten fan. She sat beside him and played poker, smoked, and chewed tobacco. He laughed in amusement at her remarks to the curious townspeople always at their heels.

"Hello, you sons of mavericks," she would call out. "When are you going to buy the drinks?" The crowd was always quick and eager to oblige.

The delight Jane felt whenever she was in the vicinity of Hickok was short lived. Within three weeks of their arrival in Deadwood, a gunman shot and killed Bill while he was playing poker. Calamity was heartbroken. After changing out of her buckskins and putting on a dress, she purchased a bottle of whiskey and went to the undertaker's office where Hickok was lying in state. She proceeded to get drunk, and she howled and cried over his body.

Under the rough, coarse exterior the brave icon preferred to display was a gentle, nurturing side that came out in times of extreme crisis. When an outbreak of smallpox threatened to decimate the Black Hills population in 1878, Calamity helped nurse the sick. She was one of the few women willing to venture into the quarantine area and care for the suffering. One of her friends bragged that Jane was "the last person to hold the head and administer consolation to the troubled gambler or erstwhile bad man who was about to depart into the new country."

Once the emergency had ended, Calamity returned to the saloons and her two favorite vices, drinking and poker.

When Deadwood became respectable and civilized, Jane moved on. It would be fifteen years before she returned to the town to visit the grave of her dearly departed Wild Bill again. During the time of her absence from the town, she claimed to have appeared briefly with Buffalo Bill in his Wild West show, met and married a man in El Paso, Texas, and had a child. Some historians doubt the validity of any of these claims.

It is a fact that in 1896 her autobiography was printed and that she subsequently embarked on a brief lecture career, touring the East Coast and sharing stories about her time on the frontier. She didn't enjoy the refinements of cities like New York and Chicago, however, and longed to be back in the West. She eventually returned to the Black Hills, taking up where she left off. She drank to excess and gambled away all of her earnings.

By 1902 Jane was broke and seriously ill. Well-meaning citizens helped pay her fare to Deadwood, where she begged to be sent. Old friends there, who remembered her kindness during the smallpox epidemic, took Calamity into their care. Her health would never fully be restored. She began having episodes of delirium and would stand in the middle of the street shouting about her time with Hickok and the daughter she believed she had.

On August 1, 1903, Calamity Jane passed away. It was almost twenty-seven years to the day Wild Bill Hickok had been shot. Although the cause of death was listed as inflammation of the bowels and pneumonia, those close to Calamity believed alcohol was the real culprit.

Deadwood residents were given the chance to pay their last respects to the frontier woman at her funeral. Many paraded past her body lying in a casket at the undertaker's parlor. A protective wire fence had to be placed over her head to stop souvenir hunters from cutting off pieces of her hair. Fifty-one-year-old Calamity Jane's last request was that she be buried next to the only man she ever loved, Bill Hickok.

Calamity Jane is nationally and internationally known. Her memory has been kept alive in numerous books and movies about her life and times. She has even been memorialized in the game of poker she loved so much: The queen of spades is often referred to as a Calamity Jane.

Kate Horony

The Hungarian Madam

"It's laughable how some people will talk. I laugh at how often I turn up dead and buried."

BIG NOSE KATE, 1883

Kate Horony pulled a crystal stopper out of a glass container filled with brandy and poured herself a drink. The svelte, well-dressed nineteen-year-old took a big gulp, then poured herself another. She slammed the second brandy back before training the derringer in her right hand on a man's body stretched out before her. Jonas Stonebreak was lying in a pool of blood with a bullet in his upper torso. He stirred a bit, struggling to lift his head off the floor. He glanced around the bedroom at the Tribolet parlor house until his blurry eyes came to rest on Kate.

She stared down at him, her eyes filled with contempt. The lifeless frame of Madam Blance Tribolet was slumped over in a chair next to Jonas. Kate motioned to the dead woman with her empty glass.

"You had no cause to kill Blance," she told him. "You're a miserable cur," she added, blinking away a tear. Kate poured another drink and Jonas tried to sit up.

"She was asking for it," he offered, spitting blood.

"No she wasn't," Kate responded pointing the gun at his head, "but you sure as hell have." She squeezed the trigger, firing off a shot that lodged a bullet in Jonas's forehead. He collapsed in a heap. Kate threw back another drink before pocketing her gun and leaving the room.

Blance Tribolet was the first madam for whom Kate Horony, better known as Big Nose Kate, had ever worked. She was more than an employer to the young woman; she was a friend and surrogate mother as well. The revenge Kate sought for the murder of her benefactor was one of many defining moments in the life of one of the West's most notorious prostitutes.

She was born on November 7, 1850, in Budapest, Hungary, and named Mary Katherine Horony. Orphaned at the age of fifteen, Kate, along with her four siblings, went to live with their guardian, Otto Schmidt, in Davenport, Ohio. Schmidt was a farmer who instantly put the Horony children to work on his property. He was a strict taskmaster who physically abused the Horonys and attempted to rape Kate. She managed to escape his attack, hitting him in the head with an ax handle and rendering him unconscious. Fearing for her life, Kate ran away. She ended up at the bank of the Mississippi with no money and, with the exception of her curvaceous figure and sharp mind, no prospects.

The river docks were crowded with boat crews, fur trappers, and gamblers, all of whom would take advantage of Kate if given the chance. She managed to avoid their pervasive come-ons and snuck aboard the steamship *Ulysses*. "Burlington" Fisher, the vessel's captain, found the teenager and questioned her about why she was there.

The trapped orphan made up numerous stories about her situation before confessing the death of her parents. She told the captain that she was trying to get to a nun's convent in St. Louis where she hoped to live. Fisher agreed to transport Kate to her destination and keep her safe during the trip. He was her brave protector and she was his appealing ward. The voyage had barely begun before the pair became lovers. Once the ship arrived in St. Louis, Captain Fisher helped place Kate in the Ursuline Convent.

Living in a convent was not the ideal setting for the strong-willed Kate, and in a matter of days she ran away. While on the run this time, she met and fell in love with Silas Melvin. The two married, settled in Missouri, and eventually had a son. A cholera epidemic claimed the lives of her husband and child less than a year after the latter's birth.

Devastated and alone, on the streets and penniless, Kate found a home at Tribolet's parlor house. Madam Tribolet introduced the disenfranchised youth to the lucrative prostitution trade. With Blance's instruction Kate became one of the house's busiest ladies.

The lifestyle suited Kate. She kept herself adorned in the finest fashions and carried herself with a modicum of class other women didn't have. Historians suggest her inviting Hungarian accent enticed a fair number of men to seek out her company. Madam Tribolet doted over her protégé and helped guide her career.

After avenging the death of her mentor at the hand of her lover, Kate wandered about the cow towns of Missouri and Kansas. In 1874 she settled in Wichita and went to work at a parlor house owned and operated by Wyatt Earp's sister-in-law, Bessie. Kate claims to have had an affair with the famed lawman, but there is no historical proof to support that assertion. Letters written between Kate and her niece alleged that Wyatt made frequent calls on the soiled dove while working at Bessie's house. Wyatt eventually ceased calling on Kate and reunited with his common-law wife, Mattie Blaylock.

Kate left Wichita in 1875 and headed to Dodge City. News of the money to be made by public women in Fort Griffin, Texas, drove her south. Fort Griffin was a popular settlement filled with cowboys, buffalo hunters, and outlaws. Doc Holliday was one of the outlaws who frequented the boomtown outside of the army post. Kate was smitten the moment she met the legendary figure.

John Henry Holliday had blond hair, a neatly trimmed mustache, and pale blue eyes seething with anguish. He had an air of sophistication about him and a devil-may-care attitude that drew Kate to him. He despised "sporting girls" with light-colored hair, painted faces, and exposed legs. Kate's dark features, voluptuous form, and determined nose, which prompted colleagues and clients to refer to her as "Big Nose Kate," better suited the outlaw. Doc was also attracted to Kate's fiery temper, fiercely independent nature, and marvelous vocabulary of curse words. Doc and Kate shared many of the same qualities, and their combination made for a rocky relationship.

By the time Big Nose Kate and Doc Holliday's paths crossed, Doc had made a name for himself as "the gambler dentist with the fast gun." Kate was starstruck and made herself available to the gambler dentist anytime, night or day.

When he wasn't with her, she would search the gambling halls and watering holes in the area looking for him. Kate was not satisfied with the occasional rendezvous. Doc was suffering from advanced tuberculosis, and Kate was determined to make him see that she was good medicine

Kate Horony, known as Big Nose Kate, was infamous throughout the West as a madam, but also for her relationship with equally infamous Doc Holliday.

A.W. BORK AND GLENN BOYER COLLECTION, SHARLOT HALL MUSEUM, PRESCOTT, ARIZONA

for him. She eventually wore him down and became a permanent fixture in his tumultuous life.

No matter who her full-time lover was, Big Nose Kate never relied on any of them for financial support. She was a self-sufficient woman who worked in parlor houses or ran her own brothel to earn a living. Doc Holliday was indeed the one man she truly loved, but he did not pay her way.

Any questions Doc might have had about Kate's devotion to him were answered one evening after a poker game involving the gambler turned deadly. Doc had shoved a knife into the chest of a fellow card player he had caught cheating. The Fort Griffin sheriff arrested Holliday and took him away to a makeshift jail at a local hotel. Kate helped Doc escape by setting fire to the building. While the authorities were preoccupied with the blaze, Kate rescued her paramour from the hangman's noose.

After Doc and Kate fled from the burning Texas hotel, they headed for Dodge City, Kansas. Once there, Doc set up a dental practice, and the two moved into Deacon Cox's Boarding House, registered as "Mr. and Mrs. J. H. Holliday." Despite their registration as man and wife, Kate and Doc were never legally married.

Doc played nightly card games with his new friends, Wyatt Earp and Bat Masterson. He began to spend less and less time with his dentistry practice, and late-night drinking brought on long bouts of sickness. Kate would stay by his side and help him get well. He loved her for it, but he also resented her good health. They fought constantly; and even though they lived as common-law husband and wife, Kate continued to work as a prostitute. Her job influenced Doc's view of her, and he oftentimes treated her as inferior, but Kate didn't care enough to quit. She liked her occupation because it provided her with her own income and she didn't have to answer to anybody.

Kate managed to make herself indispensable to Doc. He needed her. She knew how to ease him through his coughing attacks, and he actually enjoyed the volatile relationship they shared. He liked her coarseness and vulgarity. Wyatt Earp was witness to many of their fights and on several occasions suggested to Doc that he should "belt her one." Doc would reply, "Man cannot do what he wants to in this world, but only that which will benefit him."

From Dodge City the couple moved to Colorado, then on to Las Vegas, New Mexico. Doc continued to work as a dentist during the day and ran a saloon at night. Kate plied her trade at a dance hall in nearby Santa Fe. In 1879 Wyatt Earp rode into town on his way to Arizona and convinced Doc to go along with him. Kate was furious with Wyatt's interference in their relationship. She tried to talk Doc out of going, but his dedication to the Earp brothers proved to be stronger than any hold Kate had on him.

Doc joined the Earps in Tombstone in 1880, without Kate. She moved to Globe, Arizona, and bought herself a hotel with the money she had made running a parlor house in Santa Fe. By March 1881 Kate had decided she couldn't live without Doc and headed off to Tombstone. During their time apart Doc had grown paler and thinner. His bright eyes had faded to a cold, hard gray, and his head was topped by enough white hairs to make his hair appear ash blond. It wasn't long after they were reunited that their romance showed signs of the usual strain. Kate was jealous of the time he spent with the Earps and never failed to make her feelings known.

On the night of March 15, 1881, armed robbers attempted to hold up a stage near the town of Contention, Arizona. In the process they killed the driver and a passenger. An angry, drunken Kate later told Cochise County sheriff Behan and his deputy, Frank Stillwell, that Doc was responsible for the robbery and murders, and she signed an affidavit to the fact.

When Kate was sober and realized what she had done, she repudiated the statement, and the judge dropped the charges. An angry Doc gave Kate some money and a stagecoach ticket and sent her back to Globe. But she wasn't gone for good. She would return to Tombstone one more time to see her beloved Doc. She was on hand to witness the gunfight at the O.K. Corral from their room at Fly's Boarding House. Once the smoke cleared, she again went back to Globe and the thriving bordello she owned.

In 1887 Kate received word of Doc being near death, and she traveled to Colorado, where he was convalescing, to be with him. Historical records indicate that she took him to her brother Alexander's ranch near Glenwood Springs.

Doc died in a Glenwood Springs hotel on November 8, 1887. The following year Kate married George Cummings, a blacksmith. Kate left her husband shortly after they exchanged vows. It seems Cummings lacked the passion and ability to spar with her that Doc had. He later committed suicide.

Kate moved into the Arizona Pioneer's Home in 1935. She passed away five years later on November 2. The inscription on her tombstone does not list the many names she used at various times in her career as a madam and prostitute. Nor does it contain a verse or statement about her adventurous life. It simply reads "Mary K. Cummings."

Jenny Rowe

The Faro Bandit

"In a bet there is a fool and a thief."

ANCIENT PROVERB

A covey of cowboys, tinhorns, and miners clustered around a faro table at the National Hotel in Nevada City, California. A pristinely dressed dealer gingerly placed a suit of spades across a brilliant green felt game cloth. Somewhere behind him a voice called out, interrupting the sound of shuffling cards and clinking chips. All eyes simultaneously turned to face the startling beauty making her way through the men, toward the table. "Excuse me, boys," the petite woman announced. "I've got a feeling this is my lucky day."

Nineteen-year-old Jenny Rowe sashayed through the activity, smiling cheerfully as she went. She was lithe and slender and adorned in a sky-blue gingham dress that gently swept the floor when she walked. Her big, brown eyes scanned the cards on the table, and after a few moments she turned to the dealer and grinned.

"Serve 'em up," she invited. The man nodded and encouraged the other gamblers surrounding the game to place their bets. A frenzy of hands tossed their chips onto the spades across the felt.

Jenny deposited a stack of chips on the green in between the numbers. "You sure about that?" one of the cowhands next to her asked.

"I don't know a better way to put my money into circulation," she responded kindly.

The lady gambler lingered at the faro table for several hours, winning more hands than she lost. When the sun started making its eastwardly rise, Jenny cashed in her winnings. A few of the men stared dumbfounded as the dealer peeled off $500 in exchange for her chips. After leaving a generous tip with the bartender and the dealer, she slowly made her way toward the swinging doors of the saloon.

"It ain't natural," one prospector said in disbelief. "Nobody keeps laying down a bet between the numbers and wins."

"That's where you're wrong, mister," Jenny retorted. "They don't call me 'Jenny on the Green' for nothing."

Jenny was born in 1841. The exact location isn't known. Some historians cite New Orleans as her place of birth, and others list it as Atlanta, Georgia. The earliest records about the gambler's life appear in the August 1856 edition of the *Nevada Democrat*. Fifteen-year-old Jenny and her thirteen-year-old sister, Lola, were performers with Rowe's Olympic Circus. The circus was touring the Northern California gold mines, and the equestrian acrobatic siblings were part of the show.

Joseph Rowe was the founder of the company that made its debut in San Francisco on October 29, 1849. The majority of the cast members involved with the circus were orphans, including Rowe himself. Rowe acted as guardian to the teenagers who joined the program. As a sign of respect and loyalty, Jenny and Lola took on their mentor and caretaker's last name.

The arrival of Rowe's Olympic Circus into mining communities was marked by a clown or jester riding down the main street of town, playing a bugle and banging on a drum. The caravan of performers stretched for miles. Miners would lay down their shovels and leave their work at the canyons and streams and follow the show to its destination. The main acts of the circus were the horseback riders. Skilled riders and well-trained horses were judged with a critical eye, and the top equestrians were regarded as heroes of sorts.

Jenny Rowe was an exceptional bareback rider. She would lead her mare in a trot around the makeshift arena while doing back somersaults in the process. At some time during their stay in Nevada City, Jenny and her sister became ill and were bedridden. They were forced to leave the circus because of their health. The show moved on, but Jenny and Lola planned to rejoin the circus on its return through the area. They were left in the care of a Mrs. Palmer, a childless widow who doted on the sisters.

In between the time Jenny's health improved and the circus came back around, the young woman found herself smitten with a gambler named Frank Moore. Jenny was outgoing and gregarious; Moore was quiet and reserved. Their opposite personalities made for a stimulating

This 1908 photograph of a back alleyway in San Francisco's red-light district reveals the harsh conditions endured by some "crib girls."

and passionate romance. The two spent their evenings at the local saloon. Jenny sat close to the successful cardsharp, watching him gamble. Over time she developed a fondness for faro. She studied the game closely, and whenever Moore fronted her funds to place a bet, she always won.

Mrs. Palmer was appalled at her charge's behavior. She did not approve of Frank and believed gambling and carousing in a saloon led to an eternity in hell. In spite of the objections, the couple was sincere about their feelings for one another and wanted to get married. Mrs. Palmer would not consent to the union. Her disapproval did not stop the couple, however. They insisted on being together and made plans to elope. Their first attempt was thwarted by the protective sponsor. When Frank snuck into the Palmer home to liberate his would-be bride, the widow beat the persistent man over the head with a ladle.

Even though their first try at eloping was not successful, Jenny and her paramour could not be discouraged. A year after Frank's proposal they managed to get away and exchange vows. The Moores were wed in May 1858. Jenny refused to rejoin Rowe's Olympic Circus when it finally returned to the mining burg. She and her husband decided to stay in Nevada City, California, and support themselves primarily through gambling. Frank was a dealer at a popular saloon, and Jenny played faro and worked as a waitress.

In September 1859 Frank was involved in an altercation with a shady character who insisted the gambler had cheated him out of a win. The argument ended in gunplay. Frank's aim was off when he drew on the outraged man and he accidentally shot an innocent bystander. He was arrested, tried, found guilty, and sentenced to hang.

The newlyweds were mortified at the unfortunate turn of events. Jenny visited her husband daily, and the two commiserated over their tragic circumstances. Shortly before Frank was to be executed, he took his own life by swallowing a vial of poison. The authorities and townspeople speculated that Jenny provided him with the lethal substance. Neither wanted to be subjected to the humiliation of a public hanging and had sought another way out.

Many amorous men hoped to mend Jenny's broken heart, but only one captured her attention. His name was Curly Smith. Smith was an outlaw and a leader of a gang of highwaymen. Ironically, he was the same man Frank Moore had beaten at cards and attempted to gun down. Smith was fascinated with Jenny's betting habits at the faro table. She had a fondness for betting on the green instead of the actual number or face cards. He nicknamed her "Jenny on the Green," and the handle stuck.

Bored with the mundane life of gambling and waiting on tables, Jenny joined up with Smith and his men. The lifestyle suited her, providing her with a level of excitement and adventure she had never known. Smith had the brawn to back up his criminal acts but lacked the brains to plan regular attacks. Jenny had a talent for organization and in a short time transformed Curly's band of second-rate criminals into a determined gang of thieves. The Smith gang began making routine attacks on lone riders and stagecoaches traveling to and from Nevada City and Sacramento. When they weren't robbing prospectors and pioneers, the bandits were hiding out at a solitary spot in a copse of trees near the Bear River.

While Jenny was on a shopping and gambling spree in San Francisco in October 1860, Curly and his men ventured into the town of Grass Valley for a drink and a turn at the cards. Just before they reached the mining camp, they met an outbound stage and decided to attempt an unscheduled holdup. In the process of separating the passengers from their worthy possessions, they were recognized. Once the stage reached its destination, the authorities were notified and set out to apprehend the gang.

An unsuspecting Curly and his cohorts continued into Grass Valley, where they proceeded to celebrate the holdup at a saloon. Smith and a few of his men staggered out of the bar before daylight and while en route to their hotel accosted a Chinese man. Although the man was severely beaten, he managed to fight back. During the scuffle he pulled a knife from his pocket and stabbed Smith to death. The victim's actions were considered heroic, and he was commended for killing a known outlaw.

Jenny learned of her lover's demise after she returned to the Gold Country. She used the money she had made at the faro tables in San Francisco to pay for a lavish funeral. The arrangements included a silk-lined coffin, which was escorted to the cemetery by a horse-drawn hearse. Given Smith's reputation and occupation, she was unable at first to find a clergyman willing to officiate. She appealed to one of Nevada City's leading citizens, Orlando Stoddard, to help her. Moved by her impassioned request, he agreed to do what he could. Stoddard, his wife, and his sister-in-law attended the service and offered a few words on the deceased's behalf.

Jenny Rowe's whereabouts after Smith's funeral are a mystery. Historians maintain that due to her association with Smith's gang, she was forced to relocate and change her name. In November 1860 Orlando Stoddard reported that someone attempted to hold him up while he was traveling on business.

"As I passed through the place Smith and his boys were known to congregate," Stoddard relayed to a newspaper editor, "I was ordered off my horse and told to stand and deliver. Just before I dismounted I heard a woman's voice say, 'No, it's Stoddard.'" The editor indicated that "Stoddard recognized the voice as Jenny Rowe's. That was the last account ever of 'Jenny on the Green.'"

Florence Mabel Dedrick

Our Sister of the Street

"She is heart and soul in the work and has been wonderfully blessed in her efforts."

COMMENT ABOUT FLORENCE DEDRICK MADE BY THE SUPERIN-
TENDENT OF MIDNIGHT MISSIONS, ERNEST A. BELL, 1910

As the Wild West became more civilized, tolerance decreased for prostitution and the women who owned and operated houses of ill fame. Morally upright citizens spoke out against the trade, politicians drafted legislation that made the profession illegal, and missionaries ventured into parlor houses and cribs to reform the soiled doves.

Sister Florence Mabel Dedrick, a missionary from the Moody Church in Chicago, was dedicated to rescuing women from the "underworld." She believed she had been called by God to "serve her fallen sisters and persuade them to repent." She authored several articles about her experiences in helping to save women from the perils of "evil living." Their salvation was a burden that weighed heavily on her heart.

In 1910 Sister Florence wrote that she was "more than happy to share her experiences with readers everywhere." The following excerpt is from a publication she wrote entitled *For God's Sake Do Something*.

What are we doing for our tempted sisters? Are we going to let the business of prostitution have free and undisputed sway without a word of protest, blighting and ruining the homes in this fair land of liberty and freedom? Are we going to let evil exist and triumph and not rise up in arms against it?

The question, What are we doing for our sisters came up as far back as Solomon's time, but has an answer been found? No! It was only when Jesus met the woman at the well did a new life open for our unfortunate sisters. I plead with you do not draw away your skirts for fear of contamination. Remember, the Master Himself allowed a fallen woman to wash His feet with her tears and wipe them with the hairs of her head. It was a fallen woman who was first to see the omissions and deficiencies of hospitality forgotten by others. Are not fallen women included within the scope of the Master's great commission?

A woman may fall lower than a man, but this is due to her sensitive moral nature. With the conviction that she is past redemption, doors closed, no one loving her, people, yes, her own sex, ostracizing her—she becomes hopeless, desperate, and reckless. Can you blame her? Again, let me recall to your mind, Jesus Himself forgave and renewed repentant ones. Even when a woman had fallen to the depths of sin and degradation He still called her "woman."

Not every girl who leads a life of sin and shame is by any means a free person. They are in a sense a slave to sin and God is no respecter of persons and the same judgment will be hers unless she hastens home to her Father's House, where room and warm welcome awaits her. Not many doors await in her world.

An example of this is found in the case of a young girl in Colorado who, ruined, went from door to door to find someone who would befriend her. Some have one excuse, some another. All said: "We cannot take you in." Tired, discouraged, only one door open and that is the brothel door from whence she once came.

Many ask: "Who are these girls who go astray?"—having an idea that it is only the ignorant class who are down in sin. It is not so, and let me undeceive everyone on this point, though many, many of the ignorant class do go astray also. Satan is claiming our best, our VERY best girls of education, refinement, advantages and religious training. In one of the most notorious and elegant resorts, known in the red light district of Texas, there are college girls, who have had every advantage. Only lately, as I have done personal work there, did I learn that these very girls were at times in such despair as to threaten to commit suicide.

Some girls come to me when in these resorts and say: "I used to sing in Moody Church Choir." Others will tell you they went through every department of the Sunday school, some were Sunday school teachers. Members of almost every church you will find among them. When these facts are considered one cannot help but realize the need for action.

A sad incident occurred in one of Colorado's churches. Seven or eight boys, whom everyone considered pure, were found, upon investigation, to have caused the ruin of thirteen girls. One girl, in telling me how she had been led astray said she had been getting $3.50 a week for her lifestyle.

When it comes to reform there must be cooperation on the part of the state, the home and the church. What we need is a practical salvation, something more than saying: "Be ye saved." The church can do what the state cannot, and vice versa. Not only present, but future generations are in danger. Vice and crime are being flaunted, as it were, and advertised in our very faces. Every man, woman and child has a place in the battle.

It's girls whose ages are from 13 to 22 who are going astray, even as young as 9 years; deceived, betrayed, led away by the promise of making a fortune selling themselves. The conscience of these girls is by no means dead. Upon giving one my card, she said: "If I had only known it before; many tell me about being a Christian, and another world, but I never could understand it." The cry of another sin sick girl was, amid sobs and tears: "Oh! It is awful and sin has done it!"

Oh, Christian women, mothers, give recognition to the fact; yes, welcome it, that a fallen woman can be saved, and extend to her sympathy, encouragement and love! Especially let me say: "The girls of today are the mothers of the morrow, and as in the life and influence of mother rests the making of men and nations, let us, with God's help, save the girls." Knowing the price of a single soul, the burden of my heart is, that the minds of our American people may be so stirred and awakened to the existing causes of evils that are engulfing our girls, that we will each take our part, appoint ourselves as a committee of one, to do all we can to stamp out this monstrous soul scourge, and hinder and stop its further progress.

Belle Starr

The Outlaw Gambler

"Shed not for her the bitter tear, nor give the heart in vain regret. Tis but the casket that lies here, the gem that filled it sparkles yet."
INSCRIPTION ON BELLE STARR'S TOMBSTONE, 1889

Belle Starr checked to make sure the pair of six-guns she was carrying was loaded before she proceeded across a dusty road toward a saloon just outside Fort Dodge, Kansas. When she reached the tavern, she peered over the top of the swinging doors of the establishment and carefully studied the room and its seedy inhabitants. Her thin face and hawk-like nose were illuminated by a kerosene lantern hanging by the entrance.

She stepped inside the long, narrow, dimly lit room and slowly made her way to the gambling tables in the back. A battery of eyes turned to watch her walk by. Four men, engrossed in a game of five-card draw, barely noticed the woman approaching them. A tall man with an air of foreign gentility sat at the head of the table with his back to Belle, dealing cards. She removed one of the guns from her dress pocket and rested the barrel of the weapon on the gambler's cheek.

"You took $2,000 off a friend of mine," she calmly informed the cardsharp.

"I'm not in a habit of taking things, madam," the man responded. "I'm an exceptional card player."

"So is my friend," Belle offered, "and I have serious doubts that he could have been deprived of his fortune honestly."

The three other card players at the table pushed away from the scene. Belle kept her gun on the gambler.

"How do you hope to right the wrong you believe your friend has endured?" the man inquired with a sneer.

"I'll just take what's in the pot," Belle stated without hesitating.

She dropped her hand into the center of the table, and one of the other players moved as if to stop her. She removed the second six-shooter from her dress pocket and leveled it at him. No further attempts were made to keep her from raiding the pot, which amounted to more than $7,000.

"There's a little change due, gentlemen," she said as she collected the money. "If you want it back, come down to the territory where me and my boys are and get it."

Belle inched the gun away from the gambler's face but kept it cocked and ready to fire at anyone who stood in the way of her appointed goal. She tossed a saddlebag full of money over her shoulder and backed out the saloon, smiling a sly smile of contentment.

John and Eliza Shirley had wanted better for their daughter than to be a gun-toting champion of a band of outlaws that included the likes of Cole Younger and the James brothers. Belle was a headstrong woman with a penchant for crime and amoral adventures.

She was born Myra Maybelle Shirley on February 5, 1848, near Carthage, Missouri. Her father was a well-educated, wealthy innkeeper with a background in judicial affairs. His friends referred to him as "Judge," and he was sought after by many important political figures for advice on campaign support and laws that would further civilize the state.

Both John and Eliza came from genteel Southern stock. They were well-mannered people who raised their daughter and two sons to behave accordingly. As education was important in the Shirley household, Belle and her brothers were required to attend school and participate in other areas of learning as well. Belle was enrolled at the Carthage Female Academy and was taught the basic subjects along with horseback riding and music. She was a gifted piano player and had natural talent with a gun.

Being raised at a busy inn exposed Belle to a variety of rough characters and provided a less than savory education. She learned how to chew and spit tobacco, curse, and play cards. She excelled at the games of blackjack and faro. By the time Belle was fifteen, she was working several hours at the inn's tavern either playing the piano or dealing faro. Belle was a polite young woman with an innocent face, qualities that often led newcomers who challenged her to a hand to think she could be easily bluffed. The misconception enabled her to win more poker games than she lost.

A noted gunslinger among the ranks of the lady gamblers of the Old West was the horse thief Belle Starr. The tough-as-nails bandit wasn't shy about retrieving money from unsavory dealers who cheated her friends out of their winnings. Here she is pictured with her lover Blue Duck.

Rumors of an impending civil war caused a great deal of unrest with many Carthage families, and the Shirleys were no exception. Belle's brother, Edward, joined the Confederate guerilla forces and fought in a few skirmishes against free soil sympathizers before the actual war began. Belle was as strong a Southern supporter as the rest of her relatives. She wanted nothing more than to lay down her cards, pick up a gun, and fight.

When the War Between the States was declared, Edward was assigned to William Clarke Quantrill's savage military unit. It was then that Belle got her chance to serve. Quantrill's gang craved any information about the enemy. Belle was more than happy to help acquire what they needed. She rode about the town and surrounding farms under the guise of making friendly calls on neighbors and acquaintances. What she was doing, however, was gathering news from Union supporters about Yankee regiments in the area. She was learning about the supplies and artillery they had and what their movements were.

No one suspected the perky, pleasant-looking Belle of passing whatever news she learned about the Yankees on to the Rebels. Quantrill and his men called Belle their "little secret." Belle's actions did not go undetected for long. In the winter of 1862, she was arrested as a spy. She was held for a short time and then released.

Undaunted by the experience, she sneaked off to warn her soldier brother about what had happened and that the Union forces were nearby and threatening to capture all of Quantrill's troops. Belle's warning gave Quantrill's men the head start they needed to elude the Yankees.

During the time Belle was "scouting" for Quantrill, she was introduced to a few of the soldiers serving alongside her brother. Cole and Bob Younger and Jesse and Frank James were the most notable. The future outlaws applauded her efforts, and she basked in the attention they gave her. Her days of spying for the unit reached an end when the men moved on to the northeastern section of Kansas. Belle would meet up with the Youngers and the Jameses again at the conclusion of the war.

When the South surrendered to the North at Appomattox in 1865, John Shirley's business was near financial collapse. That same year he decided to sell the property and move to Texas. Eighteen-year-old Belle went with him. The Shirleys settled on an eight-hundred-acre ranch southeast of Dallas. Much to her parents' chagrin, Belle spent most of her time in Dallas playing cards. Her gambling skills were sharper than ever, and she was a regular winner. She was able to help support her family monetarily as a regular faro dealer.

Some of Belle's earnings were no doubt used to help feed renegades from Quantrill's unit who were in trouble for attacking Union sympathizers. The war was over, but many rebel soldiers could not accept the outcome. Some fled to Texas and because of their association with Edward Shirley, used the Shirley home as their rendezvous point. The James and Younger boys were frequent guests. Belle helped care for the men by cooking, entertaining them with her piano playing, and engaging them in multiple games of poker.

In 1866 Belle dealt a hand of cards to a former Confederate soldier turned bandit named Jim Reed. She was instantly smitten with the big man in his early thirties who had a weather-beaten face and a great crag of a jaw. The two were married within twenty-four hours of meeting. In spite of her father's objections and pleas for Belle to remain with him, she traveled to Missouri with her new husband. Jim made his living stealing from Union families. His illegal activities eventually brought on the law, and he was forced to run. Belle made frequent trips from their new home to visit him in his hideouts. They were now the parents of a little girl, but that responsibility did not transform the thief into a law-abiding citizen.

While Belle worked at a saloon dealing cards, Jim ran with a gang of desperados led by a violent Cherokee Indian named Tom Starr. Belle paid close attention to the players at the saloon, picking up on tips about gold and payroll shipments. Any information she had she passed on to Jim and his bunch so they could perpetrate more crimes.

In 1870 Jim murdered a man, and a warrant was quickly issued for his arrest. Believing that the law was fast on his heels, he headed for California to avoid being apprehended. Belle went back to Texas. John helped his daughter and grandchild make a new life for themselves on a nine-acre ranch down the road from the Shirley homestead.

Jim eventually sneaked back into Texas and onto Belle's plot of land to visit his wife and child. When word got out that he was hanging around, he made his way to Fort Smith, Arkansas, before authorities could catch him. Jim wasn't the only fugitive hiding out at the location. Many of Quantrill's one-time followers and a host of new renegades resided at Fort Smith as well.

Belle made a number of trips to Arkansas to see Jim and had plenty of opportunity to mix with his circle of friends, which included Tom Starr's son, Sam. Although she was loyal to Jim, Belle found Sam irresistible. Sam had feelings for her, too, but knew better than to cross the line.

Wanting to be near her husband and thrilled by life on the run, Belle accompanied Jim on several robberies. Jim and his gang traveled from Kansas to New Mexico stealing horses. On February 22, 1871, in the midst of the thievery, Belle gave birth to a second child. The Reeds named their son James Edwin. While Jim stole his way across the West, Belle watched over her children and oversaw the ranch back in Texas. In the evenings she played piano and cards at a popular Dallas saloon.

Jim's criminal activities graduated from highwayman and cattle rustler to murderer. During the first few years of his son's life, Jim had a $4,000 bounty on his head. When Belle suggested he reign in his workload a bit, he began an affair with a less demanding woman named Rosa McCommas. In August 1874 Reed's illegal endeavors came to an end when a fellow rider shot and killed him.

Two years after Jim was gunned down, Belle's father died. Alone, destitute, and anxious to be on the move, she started making plans to follow in her husband's footsteps. She sold her property in Texas and sent her daughter to boarding school in Arkansas and her son to her mother's in Missouri. She took up with members of the group of renegades Jim rode alongside. At first she merely acted as a fence or tipster in their various crimes, but eventually she helped do the actual stealing.

Her first arrest for horse thieving occurred in 1879. She was released from jail after she managed to charm the owner of the thoroughbreds into not pressing charges.

The band of outlaws she was associated with grew to include fifty men. Among them were well-known western cutthroats Jim French, Blue Duck, and Jack Spaniard. Together they picked up mavericks in Texas's Atascosa territory, rustled stampeded cattle from trail drivers on their way to Kansas, and robbed banks and stagecoaches. When they weren't engaged in dastardly doings, Belle was schooling her partners in crime in faro and five-card draw. She was such an accomplished player that her cohorts called her "the best lady gambler in the West."

When Belle and her partners were feeling particularly daring, they ventured out of hiding to enjoy an evening on the town. Some of their favorite arenas for entertainment were the saloons around Fort Dodge, Kansas. During one of their visits, Blue Duck lost all the money he had borrowed from the gang in a crooked poker game. Belle not only retrieved the funds but also a few thousand dollars more. After that incident the outlaws headed for the Starr Ranch in Adair, Oklahoma, to lay low for a while.

During the brief rest Belle became romantically involved with Sam Starr. The two were married on June 5, 1880. They spent their honeymoon in Ogallala, Nebraska, rustling cattle. A yearlong stealing spree resulted in a substantial herd of cattle and stock horses. Belle and Sam decided to drive the animals to a thousand-acre spread they purchased in Oklahoma. Once they were settled in, Belle sent for her daughter to live with them. She also bought herself a new wardrobe and a piano.

Belle didn't have much time to enjoy her fineries or renew her relationship with Pearl before federal marshals arrived on the scene. She and Sam were arrested in 1883 and escorted to Fort Smith, Arkansas, to stand trial for stealing horses. Judge Isaac Parker, the hanging judge, sentenced both Belle and Sam to a year behind bars. The pair was released after serving nine months.

The Starrs returned to Arkansas and rustling. Belle went back to dealing cards and limited the number of horses she stole. Sam robbed stages and mail hacks. He spent most of 1885 running from the law. Hard living and friendships with homicidal bandits aided in Sam's death. In 1886 he was shot and killed at a Christmas party while his cohorts looked on.

Belle was arrested two times for various crimes during a three-year span, 1886 to 1889. Each time she was released for lack of evidence. She had numerous lovers during the same time period. Among them were Cole Younger, Jack Spaniard, and Jim July. She eventually married July.

On February 3, 1889, Belle headed for Fort Smith with her new husband. July needed to be at a hearing to defend himself against a horse-stealing charge. While he was in court, Belle was going to busy herself with some shopping at the post store and then play a game of poker at the local saloon. Midway through the journey, she changed her mind and decided to return home. An unknown gunman shot the outlaw gambler off her horse. Once Belle was on the ground, the assailant shot her again in the neck and breast.

Authorities never determined the identity of Belle's killer. Some historians maintain that it was a wanted man named Edgar Watson who pulled the trigger. Others believe it was her seventeen-year-old son, Edwin. He had an explosive temper and, like his parents, was a criminal. Belle and Edwin had quarreled in public the day before she was killed. Edwin was humiliated and embarrassed by the display and vowed never to forgive her.

Belle's daughter buried her mother near the Starr homestead in Eufaula, Oklahoma. The marker over the grave includes a short verse and the usual dates of importance. Belle Starr was forty years old when she died.

Jessie Reeves and Cad Thompson

Scarlet Ladies in Texas and Nevada

"Teacher, this woman was caught in the act of adultery. In the Law Moses commanded us to stone such women. Now what do you say?"

JOHN 8:4-5

On July 12, 1900, several well-dressed guests filtered into a giant Salvation Army tent in New York City and found seats among rows of wooden crates. A steady breeze rustled the sides of the canvas enclosure but offered no relief from the oppressive summer heat. Few allowed themselves to be distracted by the uncomfortable conditions. They had come to hear a message from the former prostitute Jessie Reeves, and nothing could drive them from the setting. Once the audience was settled, the speaker approached the pulpit area.

Jessie was an attractive but hard-looking woman. The creases around her dark features made her look every bit her forty-plus years. Her eyes, though tired, reflected an inner peace. The congregation closely watched her every move. Jessie placed a well-worn Bible on a lectern and stared out at the eager crowd.

For more than an hour she shared the details of her sordid past, describing her days as a prostitute turned madam in an area known as Hell's Half Acre in Fort Worth, Texas. She described her sinful deeds and the shady characters in her association with rich detail. After painting a bleak picture of a vile past, she shared how her life had been transformed.

"I was out for my mid-day constitutional when I happened by the open doorway of a small house," she explained. "I heard someone inside singing hymns, and I was drawn to the sweet message in the music." Jessie entered the home and met the gospel minister who lived there. He told her about God and how he forgave sins. "I took the Savior into my soul that day," she happily proclaimed, "and I turned over a new leaf."

The audience was riveted by her tale of change. Hurting, troubled men and women rushed the pulpit at the conclusion of the service. Her words had turned their hearts.

Given the fact that historians have been unable to determine her real name, little has been uncovered about the early life of Jessie Reeves. Prostitutes had a habit of changing their names, in part to avoid revealing their true identity.

According to a handful of historical records, Jessie was born and raised in Spain. She arrived in Fort Worth in 1881 with her sister. Once in the United States, Jessie took on a variety of jobs, including work as a circus performer and faro dealer. Her faro-dealing days were marred with violence and injury. After losing all of his money gambling one evening, an angry cowboy shot Jessie in the chest. He accused her of dealing off the bottom of the deck. It took fifteen months for the wound to completely heal, but Jessie did survive the ordeal.

By 1885 Jessie was operating her own parlor house located across the street from the home of another famous Texas madam, Mary Porter. It was here that Jessie and her staff saw to the needs of many respectable and prominent citizens. Among the notable members of society that frequented her business was a well-known rancher and oilman who was romantically linked to Madam Reeves for many years.

Jessie was arrested several times over the course of her career. The charges ranged from operating a disorderly house to vagrancy. She was required to pay more than $600 a year in fines.

Madam Reeves's reputation was not solely tied to her profession; she was also known for being generous to the homeless, destitute children, police officers, and firemen. In the summer of 1888, a boardinghouse across from her business caught fire and threatened to destroy the entire town. Jessie sent supplies of food and blankets to the firefighters to help sustain them in their efforts. Many buildings surrounding her house burned to the ground, but Jessie's home was spared.

Virginia City, Nevada, madam Cad Thompson found herself in a similar circumstance in 1867, but she wasn't as fortunate as Jessie Reeves. Of course, Cad did not possess the benevolent spirit Jessie had, either.

This 1905 illustration aptly depicts one of the harsh realities of a life of prostitution. Entitled "Where's Mabel?" it shows a parlor-house patron enquiring of the madam about the whereabouts of one of the popular girls in her employ. The brutal answer was, "She has croaked." The upper part of the picture shows the burial of the girl in a potter's field.

Caroline (Cad) Thompson was born Sarah Hagen in Ireland in 1827. Not long after her husband passed away, Cad moved to Virginia City with her five-year-old son, Henry. As a result of the discovery of silver and gold in the area, the northern Nevada mining town was booming. Cad was a shrewd businesswoman who determined early on that she could capitalize on the lustful miners' need for women. She purchased a large, two-story brick house, moved five attractive ladies in, and invited the public to one of the town's most elegant parlor houses.

Madam Thompson's house was commonly referred to as "the Brick." It was elegantly furnished with items from San Francisco and Paris. Among the many features in the home were a piano parlor and separate rooms for each boarder.

Cad's business was always open. She hosted a steady stream of men twenty-four hours a day. The loud, drunken noises and music emanating from the home at all hours of the night prompted neighbors to level complaints to law enforcement. Cad was subsequently arrested many times for disturbing the peace and for drunk and disorderly conduct. Many times, to protest what she felt was harassment, she refused to pay the fines associated with the conviction. She instead chose to be jailed.

Cad's personal life was just as troubled as her professional one. In 1864 she became romantically involved with an Irish stonemason named John Dalton. John had been arrested for fighting as often as Cad had been for drunk and disorderly conduct. The violent tempers and stubbornness they each possessed made for a lethal combination. Cad had John arrested for assault a number of times but would eventually bail him out. The two would then reconcile and start the process over again.

One July 4, 1867, a fight between John and Cad resulted in gunplay. John threatened Cad's life, and she pulled a derringer out to defend herself. He wrested the gun from her just as the police arrived at the scene. An officer entered the home and shot and killed John. Cad claimed the officer murdered her lover, but he was found to have acted in self-defense.

Madam Thompson fought not only with her customers and romantic interests but with other prostitutes as well. Mary Livingston, a popular boarder, worked for Cad. The two got into a disagreement over a minor issue, and the argument escalated into a shouting match. Cad demanded that Mary vacate the premises. When Mary refused, the pair got into a fistfight. Cad beat the young woman to a pulp and threw her out. Mary pressed charges and a trial ensued.

Members of the male jury listened to the testimony and decided to acquit Cad. However, the men in the galley who were moved by Mary's sad tale of abuse at the hand of Cad were furious with the madam. They pledged to get even with Cad for hurting Mary. The men devised a plan to destroy Madam Thompson's place and force her out of business; they started a blaze and then sounded the alarm. Firemen responded to the growing inferno and flooded the property with water. The interior of the house was ruined. On November 18, 1866, neighbor Alf Doten noted in his journal that Cad had been the victim of a "well calculated vendetta," writing, "Some fellows took No. 1's engine about 4 o'clock this morning and washed out old Cad Thompson's whorehouse—gave her hell—created quite a consternation among the law and order portion of the community—not the end of it yet. We shall have to see who rules the city, the rough or the decent men."

Cad rebuilt the Brick and purchased two other houses. In August 1878, eleven years after the fire, her only child, Henry—a twenty-two-year-old alcoholic—committed suicide by shooting himself in the chest. He was still clinging to life when the doctor arrived to tend to his wound. Henry shunned any attempt to save him, telling the doctor, "If I had wanted to live it is not very likely that I would have shot myself."

Cad retired from the business in 1892. Historical records note that Madam Thompson and the Brick were two of the most popular attractions in Virginia City.

Belle Siddons

The Reformed Spy

"In one corner, a coarse-looking female might preside over a roulette-table, and, perhaps, in the central and crowded part of the room a Spanish or Mexican woman would be sitting at Monte, with a cigarette in her lips, which she replaced every few moments by a fresh one."
AUTHOR, LECTURER, AND FEMINIST ELIZA FARNHAM, 1854

Blood spattered across the front of the dark-eyed, brunette gambler Belle Siddons as she peered into the open wound of a bandit stretched in front of her. Biting down hard on a rag, the man winced in pain as she gently probed his abdomen with a wire loop. She mopped up a stream of blood inching its way down the crude wooden table on which he was lying.

Two men on either side of the injured patient struggled to keep his arms and legs still as the stern-faced Belle plunged the loop farther into his entrails.

"How do you know about gunshots?" one of the rough-looking assistants asked.

"My late husband was a doctor, and I worked with him," Belle replied.

"Is he going to die?" the other man inquired.

"Not if I can help it," Belle said as she removed the wire loop. She sifted through the tissue and blood attached to the instrument until she uncovered a bullet. She smiled to herself as she tossed it into a pan sitting next to her and then set about closing the man's wounds.

When Belle decided to go west in 1862, she envisioned a comfortable frontier home, a lifelong husband, and several children. But fate had other plans for the headstrong woman many cowhands admitted was a "startling beauty."

Belle's story began in Jefferson City, Missouri, where she was born sometime in the late 1830s. Her parents were wealthy land owners who made sure their daughter was well educated. She attended and graduated from the Missouri Female Seminary at Lexington. Belle's uncle was the state's governor, Claibourne Fox Jackson. She spent a great deal of time with him, traveling in elite circles that elevated the charming teenager to the toast of society.

When the War Between the States erupted, Missouri residents were divided between support for North or South. Belle and her family were Southern sympathizers, actively seeking ways to crush the Union's agenda. The attractive young Ms. Siddons fraternized with Union troops training in the area, hoping to glean valuable information from them. They were enamored with her and, in their zeal to impress her, shared too much about military plans and the positions of soldiers. Belle passed those secrets along to Rebel intelligence.

Her deceptive actions were found out by General Newton M. Curtis of the Union Brigade from New York. A warrant was issued for Belle's arrest in 1862, and she was apprehended fifty miles south of St. Genevieve on the Mississippi River. When Belle was captured she had proof of her duplicitous behavior in her possession: detailed plans of the stops of the Memphis and Mobile Railroad. The rail line was being used by the Union Army to transport supplies and weapons. When questioned about the crime, Belle proudly admitted to being a spy. She was tried, found guilty, and sentenced to a year in prison. She was released after having served only four months.

Belle left the Midwest for Texas shortly after being released from the Grand Street Prison for Rebels. She continued to support the Southern position from afar, and when the Civil War ended, she returned to the area where she was raised and became a successful lobbyist.

In 1868 she met and married Dr. Newton Hallett, an army surgeon stationed in Kansas City. When orders were handed down for the doctor to report for duty at Fort Brown, Texas, Belle gladly went along with him. The Rio Grande River bordered the rustic, lonely outpost on one side, and two African-American divisions guarded the facility. Belle's husband provided medical care to the troops, settlers, and friendly Native Americans living around the camp. She assisted him during crucial operations and learned the basics of caring for the sick and injured.

One of the most accomplished and celebrated female gamblers of the western frontier was "Madam Vestal," better known as Belle Siddons. Her lover and gambling partner, Archie McLaughlin, was eventually hanged for his involvement in illegal activites—leaving Belle a broken woman.
SEARLS HISTORICAL LIBRARY

The happy pair spent their off time visiting the nearby town of Matamoros, Mexico, where Dr. Hallett taught his pretty wife how to play poker. Belle found she had a talent for cards, in particular a game called Spanish monte. The Halletts' blissful life together was cut short when Newton contracted yellow fever and died in 1875. Belle was devastated.

Historical records differ on Belle's next move. Some maintain she quickly left Texas for New Orleans and found work dealing her favorite game. Others insist she stayed in the state, took a job teaching children how to read and write, and married a professional gambler she met on a short visit to Mexico. He too died, within the first year of their marriage. What is not disputed is that Belle Siddons turned her cardsharp abilities into a career. She honed her skills at gambling houses in Wichita,

Ellsworth, Fort Hays, and Cheyenne, Kansas. She then used her substantial winnings to open her own place in Denver.

Prospectors and businessmen who followed the news of the discovery of gold to Colorado spent time away from their strikes at Belle's gaming establishment. At this time she was calling herself Madame Vestal. The new name provided the gambling den with a sophisticated air that drew clients to the gigantic tent that housed her business. Besides free drinks, the only enticement she offered customers was a fair game.

Throughout the winters of 1875 and 1876, Belle's establishment prospered, but as the gold played out, customers moved on and business slowed. Taking a cue from the eager miners in the area, she left Denver and headed for the rich mountains of South Dakota.

A gold strike in the Black Hills saturated the peaceful territory with a collection of people who came to the emerging boomtown of Deadwood hoping to strike it rich. Belle made the move in style using a massive freight wagon called an omnibus. The interior of the spacious vehicle was elegantly decorated. Belle placed curtains on the windows and hung dried flowers on the canvas covering. The back half contained a bed and cook stove, and the front half featured gambling tables and a roulette wheel.

The journey to Deadwood took six weeks. The trail was dusty and uncomfortable, but Belle was sure the move would be profitable. While en route to the new location, Belle decided she needed a more romantic-sounding handle and changed her moniker to Lurline Monte Verde. She felt that the new name not only was considerably more enchanting, but also would be good for business because it made mention of her game of expertise.

Her grand entrance into town turned the heads of the numerous residents lining the main thoroughfare. Curious miners followed her wagon to its stopping point, and upon learning that she was a lady gambler who had come to open a gaming house there, they lifted her off the vehicle and paraded her through the camp.

Belle opened the door to her gambling parlor on June 21, 1876, and began ushering greedy patrons inside. The *Black Hills Pioneer* dedicated an entire article to the female entrepreneur, adding that she was not only a "flawlessly groomed beauty, artfully jeweled and gowned," but "a total abstainer of spirits as well."

A steady stream of customers from every walk of life strode in and out of Belle's gaming house. Soldiers, outlaws, lawmen, businessmen, and Indian scouts tried their luck at a game of poker against her. In no time she made a fortune of gold and earned a reputation as one of the finest lady gamblers in the West.

Many men would have liked to have been more to Belle than just a patron at her house, but she was steadfast against mixing business with pleasure. After meeting an ex-teamster named Archie McLaughlin, Belle reconsidered her position.

McLaughlin was a mountain of a man with an engaging smile. One evening he pulled up a chair opposite the instantly smitten dealer and promptly lost every dime he'd brought to the table. As he shrugged his shoulders and started to make his way out, Belle stopped him and offered to stake him to the next morning's breakfast. The grateful man introduced himself as Archie Cummings and promised to repay her kindness.

While Belle waited for the handsome acquaintance to reappear, he busied himself robbing stages. It turned out that her new romantic interest was the leader of a gang of highwaymen terrorizing travelers along the Cheyenne–Deadwood trail. The lack of law enforcement in the boomtown made it easy for such crimes to go on. Most residents were aware of McLaughlin's activities, but Belle was not among them.

The unsuspecting Belle welcomed McLaughlin into her gambling house a week after their first meeting. The two gambled again, and this time the thief had better luck. Before leaving he asked Belle to have dinner with him the following evening. She graciously accepted.

News of Belle and McLaughlin's rendezvous reached the bartender at her casino, and he made Archie's true identity known to his boss. Much to the young man's surprise, Belle did not seem to care. McLaughlin had so captivated her interest that nothing could persuade her from seeing him again.

In spite of McLaughlin's illegal pursuits, Belle allowed herself to fall in love with him. She was drawn to his reckless behavior. They spent a great deal of time together, and he was as taken with her as she was with him. Her misguided affections for him prompted her to share with him information she overheard in her casino. Belle made McLaughlin aware of every gold shipment passing through and of every miner with a purse full of nuggets. The gambler's lover took full advantage of the news she gave him, robbing individuals and hijacking rich stages.

Unbeknownst to either Belle or McLaughlin, the couple was being watched by the Wells Fargo chief of detectives, James B. Hume, and a hired gunman named Boone May. Boone was a frequent guest at Belle's place and had an opportunity to hear some of the same information that found its way to Belle. During one of his visits, he learned that McLaughlin and his men were planning to hold up a gold freighted stage in Whoop-Up Canyon, a run between Rapid City and Deadwood. Under cover of darkness Wells Fargo agents and a number of Boone's men rode out to the location and waited for McLaughlin to make his move.

Moments after the stage entered the tree-lined canyon, McLaughlin's gang sprang into action. They leveled their guns at the frightened driver, but before they could get a shot off, the outlaws were suddenly assaulted with a hail of gunfire coming from all around them.

McLaughlin and his gang managed to flee the scene, but not before being badly shot up and losing one rider to a bullet in the head. The surviving desperados took refuge in a hidden cabin embedded in a thick copse of trees. They nursed their wounds for more than a week before McLaughlin sent for help for the most critically injured of his men. He knew Belle was once a doctor's assistant, and he got word to her that she was needed.

Belle did not hesitate to respond to McLaughlin's plea. She pulled together medicines and supplies and hurried to meet him. Her services proved to be invaluable, as she managed to save the life of every wounded gangster in McLaughlin's company. Belle's kindness was not returned with praise and thanks, however. Instead, the ruthless thieves wanted to kill her to keep her from revealing their location. McLaughlin drew his gun and held the robbers at bay until Belle escaped the hideout safely.

Belle returned to Deadwood, and the outlaws fled the area. With the exception of one, all escaped without any trouble. The wounded man Belle had operated on was quickly apprehended by authorities, confessed to the crime, and implicated the other members of the gang in the process.

Boone and Hume formed a posse and within three months had captured McLaughlin and the other runaway bandits holed up in Cheyenne, Wyoming. The men were escorted back to Deadwood to stand trial, but before they reached their destination, vigilantes overtook the coach. The prisoners were unloaded and lynched.

When news of her lover's death reached Belle, she was so torn by grief she swallowed a small vial of poison, hoping to join him in death. The suicide attempt was unsuccessful. She sank into a deep depression and began neglecting her business and personal appearance. She turned to opium to alleviate the sadness, but to no avail. In early 1879 Belle sold her gambling house and drifted from one western town to another.

In Leadville she opened a dance hall; in Denver she ran a gaming parlor; in Cripple Creek, El Paso, and Tombstone she dealt cards and lived off her winnings. By then her addiction to opium had grown out of control, and as a result her health began to rapidly fail. In mid-1880 she moved to San Francisco, where she hoped to put her life back together. She welcomed card players to a monte table she rented at a local saloon near the wharf. Her skills as a gambler never faltered, but she spent nearly all of her winnings on alcohol and drugs.

Waves of unhappiness continued to crash around her, and she sought relief with a lethal combination of whiskey and opium. When police raided an opium den in October 1881, Belle was one of the customers arrested. The daily newspaper reported the event and noted that "she was well supplied with funds, but at death's door from alcoholism and drug use."

During an examination by the police physicians, it was discovered that Belle's ill health was not due only to her deadly vices. She also was suffering from terminal cancer. The frail lady gambler was admitted to a hospital, treated, and later died.

Belle Siddons etched her name into western folklore and is remembered by historians as a vivacious, seductive cardsharp who sacrificed everything for a desperate road agent.

Mattie Silks

Denver's Red Light Royalty

"I went into the sporting life for business reasons and for no other. It was a way for a woman in those days to make money, and I made it. I considered myself then and I do now—as a business woman. I operated the best house in town and I had as my clients the most important men in the West."

MATTIE SILKS, 1926

Mattie Silks made her way through a crowd assembled at the Lucky Chance Saloon and headed toward a wooden staircase that led to a bank of occupied rooms. Every cowhand in Colorado seemed to be drinking and gambling at the popular Denver establishment. A piano player pounded out a standard on an out-of-tune upright. Several men jumped to their feet, grabbing any public woman within reach and twirling them around. The laughing, drunken dancers paid no attention to Mattie as she pushed past them, and she was equally oblivious to them.

The stairs groaned under her heavyset form and she stumbled a bit over her long, billowing skirt before lifting the fabric to her ankles. Her attractive, round face was streaked with tears and her eyes were stern and focused. She fingered the ivory-handled pistol in the hidden pocket of her outfit, making sure the weapon was there and ready for quick use.

She paused at the top of the landing, gazing steely eyed down the long corridor. A cacophony of sounds emanated from behind the closed doors on either side of the hall. She stopped in front of the first door and listened. She did the same at the second door. Standing outside the third door she heard a man's familiar voice speaking softly to a woman, who responded with a playful giggle.

Mattie Silks, Queen of Denver's red-light district, in the finery her business sense allowed her to afford

Mattie's hand reached out for the doorknob and stopped. The urge to burst into the room was overwhelming, and for a moment she fought to curb her fury. But the muffled sound of two people kissing persuaded her to throw open the door and remove her gun in the process.

Cortez Thomson, a tall, lean, sandy-haired Texan with a handle-bar mustache, looked up at the intruder. Lillie Dab, the rumpled, red-headed woman under him, did the same. A long, awkward silence passed among the three. What to do next was anyone's guess. More out of nervousness than anything else, Cort began to laugh. Lillie followed suit, and soon the pair was in stitches over the scene. Mattie's blue eyes burned with rage. She aimed her gun at Lillie and squeezed the trigger. Lillie screamed and grabbed her head. Horrified, Lillie glanced down at the sheet, expecting to see blood; instead she saw two of her long curls lying beside her. The shot had missed her body and clipped off her hair.

Cort jumped up and scrambled for his holster and gun, which were draped across the bedframe. Mattie turned her weapon his direction and fired a shot into the floorboard next to his feet. Lillie screamed again, and Cort quickly decided against going for his gun. Mattie shot at the head-board directly behind the other woman. Lillie rolled out of bed and crawled toward the door. Mattie cocked the gun again and leveled it at the naked woman. Another round went off into the floor, barely missing Lillie. Cort hit Mattie over the head with the butt of the gun he had managed to reach. She fell in a heap beside the scuffed wood now splintered with gunfire.

Mattie Silks, "the Queen of Denver's Red-Light District," was involved in more than one violent altercation over her lover, Cort Thomson. Her fearless attempts to hold onto her man by any means possible and the sheer number of guests who frequented her palatial brothel made her one of the most renowned madams in the West.

Born in 1847 on a small farm in Kansas, Mattie was a vivacious child with massive potential. By her mid-teens she was a curvaceous brunette with sultry blue eyes and a head for business. At an early age she displayed an exceptional aptitude for managing prostitutes. By the time she was eighteen years old, she had worked as a public woman in Abilene and Dodge City. At nineteen she was managing a profitable parlor house in Springfield, Illinois.

Historians can only speculate how Mattie acquired her handle. Some suggest she took the name Silks from a man she once knew in Kansas. Others claim her love of silk material prompted clients to refer to her as Madam Silks.

After hearing that thousands of men were moving into the boomtowns and cow towns of Colorado, Mattie decided to purchase a parlor house in Georgetown. Georgetown was called the "Silver Queen of the Rockies." Twenty-three thousand dollars a year in silver was being pulled out of the hills in the area in the early 1870s. Mattie's brothel collected a large portion of those riches.

The employees at Mattie's house were considered to be the "fairest frails in town." She was particular about the women she hired and required them to meet certain standards.

"I never took a girl into my house that had had no previous experience of life and men," recalled Mattie in 1926. "That was a rule of mine. . . . No innocent, young girl was ever hired by me. Those with experience came to me for the same reasons that I hired them. Because there was money in it for all of us."

An evening of pleasure with one of her ladies cost anywhere from $10 to $200. Madam Silks claimed 40 percent of that income for herself. In exchange she provided her staff with comfortable rooms, meals, and laundry service. By 1855 Mattie was one of the wealthiest businesswomen in the trade.

Mattie's charm and success attracted numerous men, but she shunned many of their advances. It wasn't until she met Cortez D. Thomson that she decided to share her life with another. Cort was unlike the other men who had called on her. He was not a miner or a cowboy, but a foot runner. Lithe and agile, he raced challengers for large sums of money. The flamboyant racer wore pink tights and star-spangled trunks when he ran, and gamblers and the curious would turn out in droves to watch him compete. Mattie was captivated by Cort's good looks and confident air. He was drawn to her charm and money.

Ignoring the fact that Cort was married and had a child in Texas, Mattie entered into a relationship with him. In 1876 Madam Silks relocated to Denver. The prospect of making even more money enticed her to the growing town. Cort naturally followed.

Mattie's fashionable Denver brothel was a three-story brick mansion with twenty-seven rooms. It was nicely decorated and well furnished. Mattie greeted clients at her magnificent wooden front door. They were then escorted into the main parlor and serenaded by an orchestra. It was there that they had a chance to get acquainted with the beautiful and elegantly dressed boarders. Mattie kept the names of her regular customers on a list.

"I never showed that list to anyone," she told a newspaper reporter in 1926. "If a man did not conduct himself as a gentleman, he was not welcome nor ever permitted to come again. And his name was removed from the list," she concluded.

Madam Silk's parlor house was one of the most expensive brothels in Denver. Mattie's weekly income was staggering, and Cort quickly grew accustomed to an extravagant lifestyle. He and Mattie enjoyed the finest foods and wines and purchased tailor-made clothes from Paris. Cort spent a great deal of Mattie's wealth betting on horse races. He generally lost more than he won. On those rare occasions when he did win, he made small purchases for Mattie. One such item was a diamond-encrusted cross. She wore the cross on a long chain around her neck, and it became her trademark.

Historians at the Denver Museum estimate that Cort spent or gambled away more than $75,000 of Mattie's money. In addition to squandering her finances, he betrayed her with other women. The most notable was a rival madam named Kate Fulton.

Cort's relationship with the lovely and tempestuous Kate had been a simple dalliance to him, but she perceived it as much more. Kate vigorously pursued Cort and desperately tried to get him to leave Mattie. Mattie knew about the affair and for the most part was able to overlook Cort's indiscretion. On August 24, 1877, however, she was forced to deal with the persistent Madam Fulton once and for all.

Mattie and Cort hosted a grand celebration at the posh Olympic Gardens to announce their engagement—despite the inconvenient fact that Cort was still married to his first wife. Kate maneuvered her way into the party and accused Mattie of "stealing her man." The pair's verbal sparring escalated into a gunfight.

Anxious guests and townspeople lined Denver's Colfax Avenue to watch the women settle their differences with pistols. Mattie and Kate stood back to back, pistols at the ready. After pacing off a short distance, they turned and fired on one another. When the smoke cleared, the only person down was Cort.

Both Mattie's and Kate's bullets had missed their mark, but one of Kate's rounds had hit Cort in the neck. Mattie hurried to her lover's side and stemmed the flow of blood from the flesh wound with a lace handkerchief. She then escorted Cort to the hospital. Law enforcement officials took Kate to jail in restraints. Local newspapers referred to the incident as "a disgraceful occurrence of the fast element."

In a short time Cort was back on his feet. Madam Silks whisked her lover off to Kansas City for a much-needed break from the routine. She showered him with gifts and clothing and indulged herself in the finer things as well. The pair spent a great deal of time at the Overland Park racetrack, and Mattie became so enamored with the sport that she invested in a racing stable. With the exception of a chestnut gelding named Jim Blaine, all of her horses were losers.

In 1884, after a seven-year engagement, Mattie and Cort were married. Cort's first wife had died earlier that year, making him free to make an honest woman of his longtime lover. For a short time Mattie's life was good. She purchased three other parlor houses in the Denver area, all of which were extremely successful. Cort's philandering had slowed down a bit. He had, however, developed a costly but manageable gambling habit.

With business going as well as it was and with her marriage as stable as it would ever be, Mattie felt she could now pay more attention to her stable of horses. News that Cort's daughter had died, leaving behind a child of her own, halted any such plans. Cort wanted no part of the orphaned girl and refused to take her in. Mattie did not agree with her husband. She adopted the little girl, whose name was Rita, and placed her in a well-respected boardinghouse. Four years after Mattie assumed responsibility for Rita, Cort passed away. The distraught madam gave her husband a magnificent funeral, spending an untold fortune on the services and his tombstone.

At the age of seventy-seven, after more than four decades of working in Colorado's underworld, she remained the leading moneymaker in the profession. As her businesses continued to grow, so did the need to protect her ladies from overzealous clients who might harm the merchandise. With that in mind Mattie hired "Handsome" Jack Ready. Jack was a big, good-looking man who worked as not only Mattie's bouncer, but also her financial advisor. Their relationship quickly graduated from employer-employee to man and wife when the two married in 1923.

Since the turn of the century, the modern world had ever so slightly been encroaching on Mattie's trade. The Old West ideals of prostitution were tolerated less and less, and government officials were being pushed to abolish the parlor house trade. Police raids on the brothels frightened off customers, and business began to dwindle to nothing. Mattie was forced to shut her doors and sell her homes, including the famed House of Mirrors, which she had purchased from another well-known madam, Jennie Rogers.

Mattie retired to a quiet home just two blocks from one of the five brothels she had once owned. She enjoyed spending time with Jack, her adopted granddaughter, and Rita's children. When Mattie passed away at the age of eighty-one she willed her estate to her husband and Rita. Over her forty-year career, she had made millions, but when she died she had only $4,000 in cash, a few pieces of jewelry, and some property.

Madam Silks is buried at the Fairmount Cemetery in Denver under a headstone that reads, "Martha A. Ready, January 7, 1929."

Belle Ryan Cora

The Loyal Gambler

"Man is a gaming animal. He must always be trying to get the better in something or other."

HISTORIAN CHARLES LAMB, 1823

The New World gambling parlor in Marysville, California, in 1851 was filled with prospectors and sojourners eager to lay their money down on a game of chance. Patrons could choose from a variety of amusements, including roulette, dice, faro, and poker.

The New World was a grand and ornate saloon. An elaborate bar lined an entire wall and brass mountings accentuated the gleaming countertops. Imposing mirrors clung to all sides of the enormous entryway, and paintings of nude women relaxed in beauty prostrate loomed over the patrons from the walls above.

Madame Belle Ryan, a voluptuous creature with dark hair, hazel eyes, and a fair complexion, sauntered down the stairs, surveying the guests who had gathered. Men scrambled for a place at the tables; their gold dust and gold nuggets had been exchanged for the chips they tossed onto the green felt—bets for the lucky cards in their hands.

Charles Cora, a handsome brute of a man with black hair and a thick, trimmed mustache, caught Belle's eye. He was very nicely dressed. From the bowler hat on top of his head to the polished black boots on his feet, he exuded style and confidence. Charles was seated at a table in the corner of the room, dealing a hand of poker to four men around him. The pile of chips in front of Charles was proof that he'd had a successful evening. He turned to look at Belle and gave her an approving nod. She smiled back at him, then noticed a handful of cavalry soldiers standing just inside the saloon. Charles spotted the men too and motioned slightly for Belle to go over to them. She winked and proceeded obligingly.

The wide-eyed troops admired the beautiful Belle as she strode their way. "Why don't you come on in and join the fun. Have a drink, sit in on a game or two?" she purred invitingly.

"We aren't much for gambling, ma'am," one of the young soldiers shared. "We just got our pay and thought we'd stop in for one shot of whiskey and then be on our way."

Belle slowly approached the uniformed man and stopped uncomfortably close to his face. The soldier breathed in her perfume and then glanced away, shyly. "But it's so early," she said, smiling. "Have a drink, play a hand of faro, and then we'll dance," she persuaded.

"I guess we can stick around for a little while," the enchanted young man offered.

Belle escorted the troops to the bar and had the bartender serve them a glass of whiskey. "That one's on the house," she assured them. She then locked arms with a pair of the soldiers and ushered them to the faro table. They obediently sat down, and Charles tipped his hat at the new players. "I'll be back in a bit for my dance," Belle whispered in their ears.

As Belle walked away the bartender served another round of drinks to the soldiers and Charles started dealing the cards. By the time Belle returned to the table, the troops had lost their entire wages. They took a turn with her on the dance floor and then lumbered out of the establishment, dazed and disappointed.

Occasionally Belle was the one that dealt the cards, but her main contribution to the gambling industry was luring players to the game and building their confidence. Belle and her partner, Charles Cora, made hundreds of thousands of dollars off unsuspecting marks who believed they were better than the professional gamblers luring them to the tables.

Belle Ryan Cora was born in Baltimore in 1832; her parents named her Clara Belle. Her father was the minister of a small parish, and the home life she had with her doting mother and young sister, Anna, was idyllic. At seventeen she fell in love with a distinguished older gentleman and became pregnant. After learning the news the child's father abandoned them. Desperate and ashamed, Belle fled to New Orleans to have her child. The baby died shortly after being born, leaving Belle despondent and alone. While wandering the streets of New Orleans contemplating

The popular Belle Ryan Cora's house on Waverly Street in San Francisco
CALIFORNIA HISTORICAL SOCIETY

her life, she met a kindly woman who took pity on her situation and offered to help.

Belle recognized the woman as a known madam in the city. She was fully aware of the kind of assistance being presented, but she felt her options were limited. After accompanying the woman to her parlor house, being fed and provided a new wardrobe, Belle accepted her offer of work. In a matter of only a few months, she was earning more than any other woman in the city.

When Charles Cora, a well-known New Orleans gambler, spotted Belle he was instantly smitten. She was equally taken with him. The two began spending time together and in a few weeks were inseparable.

Once the news of the California gold rush reached Charles, he decided to try his luck in a place rich with glittering finds. With Belle by his side, he boarded a steamship bound for San Francisco. Charles and Belle weren't the only ones with a dubious past making the trip. The vessel contained more than forty gamblers and ladies of the evening. Personalities clashed during the voyage. The scruples of such a motley group of passengers were questionable or nonexistent. When they weren't cheating one another at a game of poker or faro, they were conning law-abiding travelers out of their possessions or blatantly stealing from others.

Charles was one of two thieves who got caught trying to take writer Edward L. Williams's purse filled with money. On December 11, 1849, Williams recorded the incident in his journal.

I was hanging in a hammock near the bow, alongside a row of bunks. Not long after falling asleep I was awakened by a volley of curses and a loud "Get out of here!" There followed more coarse and vile oaths and the threat: "If you don't get out, I will cut you down. You are keeping the air from me!" I didn't move. One of them I recognized as Charles Cora removed a large knife from his pocket. Just then, on the other side of his hammock I saw a pistol gleaming in the moonlight and the man holding it said, "You attempt to cut the boy down for his purse before me and I will blow a hole through you, you infernal blackleg Southerner. I know you, you used to run a gambling game at New Orleans and you robbed everybody. Get away from that boy!"

The confrontation between Charles and the competing robber intensified as the voyage continued. Angry over the thwarted attempt to steal a bankroll to gamble with, Charles and his cohorts took to bullying the passengers. He caused so much trouble that the ship's captain had him and his partners in crime placed in irons.

Belle and Charles arrived in San Francisco on December 28, 1849. The gambling team then boarded a stage for Sacramento. The river city was the location for some of the territory's biggest poker games. The price to sit in on one particular game was $20,000. Belle put up the money and Charles played. He won a sizeable amount in one hand, but his luck quickly changed and he lost it all. Belle fronted him an additional $60,000 to stay in the game, but he was unable to turn things around. He then solemnly vowed he would never again play with a woman's money.

The lovers left Sacramento and made the rounds at the various mining camps in the foothills. They set up games at makeshift saloons, and Belle lured prospective gamblers in for Charles to fleece. Once they had made up the losses they incurred in Sacramento, they moved on to Marysville and opened a gambling den called the New World.

There were no limits on the bets taken at the tables at the New World. One prospector recalled that "Charles Cora himself laid down a bet of $10,000 in one hand of five-card draw. He won his bet too."

Once the gaming house was established and earning a profit, Belle sought to expand the enterprise. In April 1851 she traveled to Sonora. The booming mining town had a population of five thousand people and was in desperate need of additional entertainment. Using the name Arabelle Ryan, Belle purchased a house of ill repute. She expanded the business to include gaming and developed a reputation as a confidence woman, gaining clients' trust to entice them into games of chance. She called the combination brothel and gambling den the Sonora Club.

The business was a profitable venture. Charles followed after his paramour and dealt cards for her. By the end of 1851, Belle and Charles had earned more than $126,000 from their combined businesses in Sonora and Marysville. The gamblers used their substantial holdings to move their trade to San Francisco.

Although Charles and Belle were not married, she took on his last name when they relocated to the City by the Bay. The pair operated out of a three-story wooden building that had two entrances. Belle decorated the combination bordello and casino with the finest furnishings and accoutrements. When the Coras opened the doors to the business on November 17, 1852, patrons reported that "it rivaled the finest residences in the city." Customers included politicians, entrepreneurs, and gambling professionals. They were treated to free champagne and hors d'oeuvres, the most beautiful women in the trade, and liberal tables with a new deck of cards or dice each night.

A description of the Cora House included in a manuscript written in 1855 by historian Frank Soule provides a good indication of the establishment's popularity.

In the fall of 1855, Belle and Charles hosted a party designed to attract high rollers to the den. The evening the couple selected for their soirée fell on the same night Mrs. William Richardson was having a get together. Mrs. Richardson and her husband, a U.S. Marshal, were unhappy with the lack of male attendants at their event. When they learned that their invited guests chose to go to Belle's place, the marshal and his wife were furious.

The previous year antigambling laws had been passed by California representatives, and all such establishments were to have been shut down. Charles Cora could no longer practice his profession legally. The Richardsons suspected the party at Belle's place had actually been a private game in which Charles was the dealer. Mrs. Richardson and the marshal vowed to monitor the activities at the Cora House and catch the pair in the act of breaking the law. When Charles learned of the Richardsons' plan, he informed Belle. A bitter feud between the couples erupted.

On November 5, 1855, the Coras and the Richardsons attended a play at the American Theatre. The two couples were placed in balcony seats in close proximity to each other. When the Richardsons learned that the Coras were at the same performance, the marshal demanded that the theater management throw the "low moral fiber duo" out. When the manager refused, the Richardsons left.

Over the next week Charles and the marshal exchanged insults and derogatory remarks. Whenever their paths crossed tensions escalated into threats. Finally the two met on the streets to settle things once and for all. The gambler shot Marshal Richardson in the head with a derringer, killing him instantly.

Charles was arrested and thrown into jail. Many of the townspeople who admired the marshal were outraged and demanded that Cora be hanged immediately. Belle rushed to her common-law husband's aid and hired two attorneys to represent him. The cost of their combined retainer was $45,000.

While Belle fought to prove that Charles acted in self-defense, a vigilante committee was being organized. Leaders of the group planned to overtake the jail and exact their own justice. Initial attempts to break into the facility and remove Charles were thwarted. He was arraigned on December 1, 1855, and the trial was set for early January. Belle was not content with merely purchasing good counsel, and she turned her attention to the witnesses who claimed to have seen Charles brutally gun down the unarmed marshal. Belle met with an eyewitness to the shooting and offered her money to change her story. When that didn't work Belle threatened to kill her. Neither approach convinced the witness to retract her accusation.

Charles's trial began on January 3, 1856. Shortly after a jury was selected, Belle attempted to bribe a select few of them. Her efforts were fruitless. No one would agree to side with the unpopular couple. The court was made aware of Belle's behavior but decided against any legal action.

The trial was lengthy and the prosecution played up the "devious" characteristics of Charles and Belle, referring to the pair as "shady gamblers with sinfulness in their lives." The defense argued that their morals weren't on trial and that whatever "sinfulness there was in Belle's life, it was far outweighed by her fidelity to her man."

The jury deliberated for forty-one hours but failed to reach a verdict. While Charles awaited a second trial, the public at large grew more and more incensed at the lack of outcome. Believing that Charles would get away with murder, the vigilante committee stormed the jail and escorted him to a secret area to be hanged. A blindfolded Belle was brought to the location of the execution. The tearful madam asked if one of the clergymen there would marry her and Charles. Minutes before Charles was put to death, the two were legally wed.

Heartbroken and inconsolable, Belle Cora retreated to her bedroom at the gambling den and remained tucked away in the house for more than a month. Belle emerged a changed woman. She sold the business and moved to a small house with only a few servants as company. She used her considerable financial holdings to support local charities and help children obtain a higher education. She died in San Francisco on February 17, 1862, having given away the bulk of her fortune. She was thirty years old.

Rosa May

The Outcast's Friend

"Unattached females arrive in the boomtowns in a dead heat with the saloons. They entice men into small back rooms for amorous interludes, and split the fees with the saloon owners. I believe they are void of all human emotion and only love money."
HARRISON PHILLIPS, *A MINER'S MEMOIRS*, 1852

Rosa May sat beside the bed of a dying miner and wiped the sweat off his feverish brow. She looked around his rustic, one-room cabin, past the sparse furnishings, and fixed her eyes on a tattered photograph of an elderly man and woman. "Those are my folks," the man weakly told her. "They're in Marshall County, Illinois. Where are your folks?"

The question stunned Rosa. No one ever asked about such things. No one ever asked her much at all. Conversation wasn't what men were looking for when they did business with her. Rosa glanced out the window at a couple of respectable, well-dressed women. They watched her through the clouded glass, pointed, and whispered. She knew what they were saying without hearing it.

Rosa was just one of a handful of "sporting women" living in Bodie, California, in 1900, and she knew what people thought of her. It had bothered her in years past, but not by the turn of the century. It was an occupational hazard she'd learned to live with.

"Don't you have people anywhere?" the miner asked. Rosa dabbed the man's head with a cloth and smiled. "I don't know anymore," she answered. "If I did have they'd be back in Pennsylvania."

Rosa's parents were Irish—hard, strict people. Rosa had dreamed of the day she would be out of their puritanical household. She had left home in 1871, at the age of sixteen, and soon found there weren't many opportunities for a poor, petite, uneducated girl with brown eyes and dark, curly hair. She ended up in New York, hungry, homeless, and eager to take any job offered. The job offered was prostitution, and five years later she went west with other women of her trade, hoping to make a fortune off the gold and silver miners.

Prostitution was the single largest occupation for women in the West. Rosa hoped to secure a position at a posh brothel with crystal chandeliers, velvet curtains, and flowing champagne. The madams who ran such places were good to their girls. They paid them a regular salary; taught them about makeup, manners, and how to dress; and required them to entertain only a few men a night. If a high-class brothel wasn't available, Rosa could take a job in a second-class house and work for a percentage of the profits, turning as many tricks as she could each night. If all failed, she could be a streetwalker or rent a "crib" at a boardinghouse—a tiny, windowless chamber with an oil-cloth draped across the foot of the bed for customers in too big of a hurry to take off their boots.

Rosa arrived in Virginia City, Nevada, in 1875 and went to work for a madam known as Cad Thompson. Cad was a widow who ran several parlor houses in town, including a three-story structure called "the Brick." Cad and Rosa became fast friends, confiding in one another and talking about meeting their Prince Charming. "Whores dream of falling in love, too," Cad frequently told Rosa.

In 1878 Rosa met a man she hoped would be her prince. His name was Earnest Marks. He was twenty-two, tall, and well dressed, with a slight mustache. He told Rosa she was "handsomer in my eyes than anyone I know." The two found in one another what they most desired—companionship and comfort.

Erni tried hard but had difficulty finding steady employment. He did whatever jobs he could find: mining, bartending, bill collecting. Most women would not have seen Erni as Prince Charming; he was a heavy drinker and a regular at brothels all over the area.

If Rosa had any thoughts that Erni would settle down with one woman, marry her, and save her from the life she led, Cad helped change her mind. Marriage didn't automatically mean that you would be living with your spouse or retire from prostitution, Cad would remind her.

Rosa May, soiled dove with a heart of gold
COURTESY OF BODIE STATE PARK, BODIE, CALIFORNIA

Oftentimes men who married prostitutes expected them to keep working. Cad believed Erni would expect no less from Rosa.

Rosa was not convinced. Erni always referred to her as his "little girl" and made her feel protected. She believed that if they were married, he would take care of her. But Erni Marks would never take Rosa May for his bride. The social stigma was too much for him to bear.

Rosa tried not to think about that as she sat in the dim room with the dying miner. She removed a pad of paper and a stump of a pencil from her oversize handbag and laid them on her lap. She had written letters for other Bodie miners suffering from pneumonia and was ready to write one more for the prospector next to her.

Rosa wrote letters constantly, most often to families in the East. She would write to tell them of their relatives who died. It wasn't uncommon for a soiled dove to be murdered by a customer. Sometimes the women were so desperate to escape life at a brothel that they would kill themselves. Rosa felt an obligation to let their families know when their loved ones passed on. She believed they'd want to know what had happened, even if their loved ones were prostitutes.

Letters played an important part in Rosa and Erni's relationship; they exchanged many during the years they were together. Erni eventually left Virginia City and took a job in Gold Hill, a town some twenty miles away. Rosa and Erni wrote each other every three days. Rosa missed Erni terribly. He would travel to see her as often as time and money permitted, but in between visits she worried about his drinking and was jealous of his carousing. She knew he kept company with other prostitutes and madams.

Erni had a tremendous sexual appetite and found it impossible to be monogamous. Many times Erni's letters to Rosa were written to ease her worry about his alcoholism and assure her of his true feelings.

February 2, 1879
Dear Rosa,

I was happy to get your letter today. I am being a good boy, love, and I shall continue to be. I am doing well, but am a little shaky. I suppose

it is because I drink so little now, but I feel better for it and I look bet-
ter too. No! Pet, I have not been with another. I have no interest in
anyone but you.

Love and kisses for my dearest Rosa.
Erni

But Erni was not faithful to Rosa. He had many lovers. Even if that
hadn't been the case, he likely would have never publicly acknowledged
his love for her. To admit being in love with a prostitute was scandal-
ous, and Erni was afraid that neither he nor his family could endure the
humiliation. Besides, his inability to hold down a job for any extended
period of time had already left him with a poor self-image. He denied
rumors that he and Rosa were a couple. When word of his denial would
get back to Rosa, he would rush off another letter to reassure her of his
love.

January 7, 1879
Dear Rosa,

You sweet, dear baby. I got your letter just fine. How could you believe
that I might be moved by what others say about you and I. There's
nothing to it. I don't let them bother me at all. You are my love.

Forever,
Erni

Rosa moved back and forth between parlor houses in Virginia City
and Carson City, Nevada, following the gold and silver strikes. When
the precious metals were played out in both towns, fewer and fewer men
visited Rosa, and those who did wouldn't pay.

Erni moved to Bodie, California, to work for his brother in the whole-
sale liquor business. He curtailed his visits to Rosa, who wrote him about
how much selling liquor troubled her. She didn't think his struggle with
alcohol could get better working in that profession. Rosa broke off their

relationship and vowed never to write another word to him, but Erni's letter in response changed her mind.

April 17, 1879
My Darling Rosa,

Your letter sounds as though you feel hurt . . . I am sorry to see you feeling as you do . . . I am sorry I was not on the train to meet you, but I hope you will think no harm in it and not feel hard toward your baby for I meant not to fool you and would not willingly disappoint my pet for any consideration. Why do you say goodbye? For today there is no hard task, no burden that I would not bear with grace, no sacrifice I could name or ask that were granted could I see your sweet face. Oh, Rosa how can you think for a moment that goodbye?

Always,
Erni

Rosa and Erni reconciled, and the letters began to flow freely between the two lovers once again. Erni shared his feelings of insecurity with Rosa, and she shared her feeling of loneliness with him. They encouraged each other and held each other accountable for their misdeeds. Rosa chastised Erni for his drinking, and he would always apologize and promise to do better.

They also shared stories about their illnesses. Rosa suffered from chills and fever, a condition that originated when she lived in the cold, flimsy parlor houses in the East. Erni had gout and a venereal disease.

In 1891 Rosa moved to Bodie. Remote as it was, Bodie was still a booming gold town, and she thought business would be better there and she'd be close to Erni. She moved into a white house in the red-light district. She kept a neat brothel and listed her occupation with the census as "seamstress."

Erni was happy Rosa had moved to town. Under cover of darkness he would make his way back and forth from Rosa's home to the saloon where he worked. In the light of day Erni insisted his relationship with Rosa was strictly professional.

Rosa eventually became sick caring for pneumonia-stricken miners. She died in 1911 at the age of fifty-seven. Erni couldn't afford the monument he had promised Rosa he would put on her grave, and no one took up a collection to remember the gentle kindness of Rosa May. She was buried in the outcast cemetery with a simple wooden cross marking the spot.

Erni lived out the rest of his days working in his bar. In 1919 Prohibition drove him out of the saloon and wholesale-liquor business. His brother supported him until his death in 1928.

Laura Bell McDaniel

Courtesan of Colorado City

"The West is overrun with bawdy houses and soiled doves."
GOLD MINER CHARLES BARTLETT IN A LETTER HOME TO HIS
FAMILY IN VIRGINIA, 1872

Madam Laura Bell McDaniel's broken body lay in a ditch beside a snowy thoroughfare conjoined with the twisted rubble of what was once her pristine Mitchell sedan. It was late January 1918 when the notorious soiled dove's car crashed just outside Castle Rock, Colorado. Laura's twenty-seven-year-old niece, Laura Pierson, had been driving the vehicle; she was thrown from the sedan when it overturned. A blind family friend, Dusty McCarty, was in the car with the women. He survived the accident but sustained several bruises and cuts.

By the time Laura Bell McDaniel was transferred to Memorial Hospital in Colorado Springs, news of the plight of the woman known as "the Queen of the Colorado City Tenderloin" had already reached clients and citizens where she lived and worked. Many were saddened by the news, and some believed Laura's car might have been forced off the road by those who wanted her house of ill repute shut down.

Laura was born near Buffalo Lick, Missouri, on November 27, 1861. Her parents, James and Anna Horton, were farmers who made sure their children were well educated. At the age of nineteen Laura married Samuel Dale from nearby Brunswick, Missouri. The two had become acquainted when Laura's father took the family buckboard to Samuel's father, a wagon maker, to be repaired. The couple left the Midwest shortly after they were married, traveled to Colorado, and settled in a newly established railroad town called Salida. Sam and Laura welcomed a baby girl into their lives in 1884 and named her Eva Pearl Dale. Marriage and fatherhood did not sit well with Samuel, and he left a few months after his daughter was born.

Faced with the challenge of raising a child on her own and with no viable employment opportunities, Laura ventured into the business of prostitution. She purchased a home close to the house where her mother lived. Her mother, Anna, had relocated to Colorado when Laura and James began having marital problems. Anna opened a boardinghouse, which she ran with Laura's two younger sisters.

One of Laura's regular callers was John Thomas "Tom" McDaniel. The two spent a considerable amount of time together and traveled to Leadville on occasion in the winter. It was during one of those trips that Laura's home caught fire and burned to the ground. Foul play was immediately suspected, and one of Anna's boarders was accused of setting the blaze. Morgan Dunn was considered to be a man of questionable character by most Salida residents, and he was quite enamored with Laura. He was extremely jealous of the relationship she had with Tom.

Laura had insurance to cover the home in case of a fire. While waiting for the insurance check to arrive, she moved to a house near the red-light district of town. She and Tom continued to see a lot of one another and eventually became engaged. They were married on April 7, 1887. Less than a week later, the duo were involved in a scandal that threatened to end their lives together.

On April 13, 1887, the day before the newlyweds were scheduled to go on their honeymoon, Laura confided in Tom that Morgan had tried to kiss her. Tom was furious to hear that someone had tried to take advantage of his wife. "Why didn't you kill the son of a bitch?" he shouted at Laura. Tom decided to confront Morgan about his actions, and Laura was unable to reason with him. The pair arrived at Anna's home and charged inside, Tom ready to fight the forward boarder and Laura trying to intercede. Morgan, who was eating dinner when Tom approached him, was initially nonplussed about the incident. When Tom continued to press him on the issue, he became belligerent. A yelling match ensued, and before it became physical, Laura managed to talk her husband into leaving and going home.

Tom didn't stay home, however. He returned to have it out with Morgan. The two got into another battle of words, and Morgan suggested they settle their differences in another way. When Morgan placed his hand on

Gambling parlors like this re-created version at the Colorado History Museum in Denver lured Old West travelers inside with tasteful decor; an array of alcohol; a clean, unmarked deck of cards; and a stunning woman to blow on the dice for good luck.

THE DENVER PUBLIC LIBRARY, WESTERN HISTORY COLLECTION, X-757

his hip pocket, Tom pulled out a gun and shot him five times. Morgan collapsed at Tom's feet, dead.

The sound of the gun firing drew the attention of the next-door neighbors, and they hurried to the scene. According to the May 20, 1887, edition of the *Salida Semi-Weekly Mail*, they found Tom standing inside the front door. His wife and mother-in-law were holding on to him and crying, "Oh, Tom!" The neighbors told police that Anna screamed, "Why did you do that?" Tom was arrested and tried for his actions, but the court found him not guilty. He claimed that he had acted in self-defense.

The residents in and around Salida doubted not only Tom's version of the story but also the motive Laura offered for why he went to see Morgan. Not everyone believed he was driven by jealousy alone. It was suspected that Tom killed Morgan to keep him from ever talking about setting fire to Laura's home. Citizens were convinced Tom and Laura hired Morgan to burn the home in exchange for a sizable insurance check. The *Salida Semi-Weekly Mail* reported that Morgan was unarmed the night he was shot. The article also noted that he had been recovering from a broken arm and collarbone, injuries he had sustained in a bar fight.

When Morgan's wife, who was living in New York at the time of his demise, eventually learned about her husband's death, she wrote the judge that presided over Tom's case to ask him specifics about the killing. She learned that Morgan had run afoul of the law on occasion and had been laid to rest in a pauper's grave without a service or friend to see him off.

Tired of the idle gossip that surrounded the case, Laura and Tom decided to give an interview to the editor of the *Salida Semi-Weekly Mail* and correct the issues that were being talked about. Far from clearing up matters, the interview prompted more questions. The McDaniels told the paper that Morgan had removed his coat and placed it on the bed prior to the shooting. Actually, police found the victim in his coat. As for Morgan placing his hand on his hip pocket, Laura's mother claimed that never happened. The McDaniels told the newspaper editor that Anna was wrong.

Not long after the trial, Tom and Laura left Salida and somewhere along the way parted company. By 1888 Laura was living in Colorado City alone. She purchased a home to use for business and began referring to herself as Mrs. Bell McDaniel.

Laura's brothel was one of the most spectacular in town. It featured a ballroom, chandeliers, and expensive furniture. She had servants, a bartender, and a cook. Laura entertained powerful, well-known, and wealthy individuals.

Laura and many of the other soiled doves in Colorado City conducted themselves in public with restraint, moderation, and dignity.

When the women took walks and shopped, they confined themselves to the red-light district. There was no solicitation, and they were polite to everyone they met. Laura was known for being generous with her earnings. She frequently gave money to the homeless and helped them find a place to live; she also gave to charities that provided food and clothing to the needy.

Anna Horton was never too far from her daughter. She moved from Salida to Colorado City in 1890, and mother and daughter visited often with one another. Laura sent her daughter, Eva Pearl, to a boarding school. She wanted her to have an education and to choose a different path in life than she had. It is not known if either Laura or Anna visited Eva while she was away or even where exactly Eva attended school.

Many colorful characters paraded in and out of Laura's life and business. John "Prairie Dog" O'Bryne, a hack driver and brakeman for the Atchison, Topeka and Santa Fe Railroad; notorious female gambler Minnie Smith; and mining and real estate magnate Charles Tutt were just a few.

In June 1893 Laura filed for divorce from Tom. The marriage was officially dissolved four months later. By the turn of the century, Laura's mother, Laura's sister Birdie, Birdie's husband, and their infant son were all living together in the same home down the street from Laura's house. In 1901 Eva Pearl was also a resident in her grandmother's home.

Laura's reign as "Queen of the Colorado City Tenderloin" did not falter in the early 1900s. Her business did, however, suffer from the usual problems associated with running a bordello: unruly patrons, rivalries with competing houses, and desperate employees who tried to kill themselves. There was also the occasional tussle with law enforcement. According to the April 30, 1903, edition of the *Colorado Springs Weekly Gazette*, Laura, along with eight other women, were arrested for prostitution, and an indictment was returned to a grand jury against her for running a house of ill repute. She gave a bond in the sum of $500.

"Evidence before the grand jury is to the effect that the houses have been run under the protection of the authorities of Colorado City who have collected monthly fines from each house," the *Weekly Gazette* article read. "The arrests were entirely unexpected; an unsuccessful attempt to escape was made. Other and sensational developments in regard to the morality of the county, it is rumored, will follow."

After making a court appearance in June 1903, Laura decided to move her business to Cripple Creek. Less than two years later she returned to Colorado City. In 1905 her mother died and she relocated again to Cripple Creek, but she kept her place in Colorado City. She was now running a bawdy house in both locations.

Historians speculate that Laura changed addresses multiple times because laws against prostitution were strictly enforced in the early 1900s. Upstanding citizens did not tolerate women of ill repute, especially those who were warned to vacate their premises but chose to stay. Madams who rebelled against the law were sometimes beaten and their homes were burned to the ground. Laura had suffered through many fires, and regardless of the reasons for those fires she always rebuilt.

Laura's most famous house of ill fame was called the Mansion. The grand brick bordello cost more than $10,000 to build. Colorado City residents were outraged that Laura dared to have another house constructed. According to the May 7, 1909, edition of the *Colorado City Iris*, her actions were viewed as an attempt to reinvigorate the red-light district, which most people hoped was gone for good.

In February 1911 Laura married Herbert N. Berg, the financial editor of the *Colorado Springs Gazette Telegraph*. Her lifestyle did not change after she wed, however. She continued as a madam and even placed an ad in the *Gazette Telegraph* announcing that she was still open for business. She discreetly referred to herself in the ad as a "keeper of furnished rooms." Local authorities paid several visits to Laura's house and fined her for running a brothel. From 1909 to 1911 she paid more than $400 in fines for "keeping a disorderly house."

Herbert died in mid-1916, and the following year law enforcement concentrated their efforts on ridding the community of Laura's business. On November 20, 1917, the Colorado City police served Laura with a warrant to search her property. She wasn't sure what they were looking for and was surprised when they produced thirty-four bottles of liquor reportedly stolen from the home of one of Colorado Spring's most wealthy citizens, Charles Baldwin.

Laura was arrested for "receiving stolen liquor." She was taken into custody and charged. Bail was set at $1,500, and her trial was scheduled for January 18, 1918. Laura retained a pair of attorneys with a substantial background in representing soiled doves. James Orr and W. D. Lombard asked the court for additional time to prepare their client's case, and the request was granted. The court date was moved to January 24.

Witnesses for the prosecution consisted mainly of police officers and detectives. They alleged that on November 12, 1917, Laura Bell purchased several bottles of stolen liquor. Among the items she supposedly bought were Gordon's gin, champagne, and high-grade whiskey. Charles Baldwin, the so-called victim, did not appear at the trial. He had been called out of town and did not know when he would be returning.

Laura's longtime friend Dusty McCarty came forward to testify on her behalf. When he took the stand, he explained to the court that the liquor had been planted at her home. Dusty maintained that two men who frequented her business were the real culprits. The case against Laura was dismissed.

The day after Laura's case was closed, she, her niece, and Dusty decided to take a drive to Denver. Laura Pierson was driving when the car jumped off the pavement at forty miles per hour and flipped over. Rumors abounded that the Colorado City police were behind the crash. Both Lauras died from injuries received in the wreck. Some believed that Laura Bell paid the ultimate price for defying the law in court.

After an elaborate funeral Laura was buried at Fairview Cemetery in Colorado City. Her niece was laid to rest beside her. Laura's daughter was the sole heir of her estate, which amounted to more than $15,000 in cash and property.

Laura Bell was fifty-six when she passed away.

Mary Hamlin

Mary the Owl

"The gambler is a moral suicide."
REVEREND CHARLES CALEB COLTON, 1832

On July 9, 1871, two ragged, down-and-out prospectors walked into the Bank of California in San Francisco and approached a dignified-looking clerk waiting behind a giant oak desk. The two hungry-looking men quietly inquired about renting a safe deposit box. The clerk eyed the unkempt miners suspiciously before answering. "Why would you need such a box?" he asked impolitely. The men exchanged a knowing look and, after glancing around the room to see if anyone was nearby, dropped a buckskin bag in front of the clerk. Just as the clerk was reaching for the bag, it tipped over and several sparkling diamonds toppled out. The clerk's eyes opened wide. "Diamonds," he gasped. "Where did you get them?"

"Oh, up in the mountains," one of the men said casually. "We sort of figured we better have a safe place to keep them while we go up and get more."

The clerk gladly rented them a safe deposit box. The two put the sack inside it and sauntered toward the bank exit, staring around them at the splendor of the marble interiors.

Across town Mary Hamlin, a young woman with a slim figure, a round, gamine face, and golden blond hair, peered expectantly out of her upstairs hotel room window. When the two miners appeared on the dusty thoroughfare below, she opened the glass, casually took a seat on the sill, and glanced down at the men. She caught the prospectors' eyes, and they nodded pleasantly to her as they passed. Mary batted her blue eyes at them while twirling a long curl of her hair around her finger. A devilish grin spread over her face and she laughed to herself as if she knew something the rest of the world didn't.

A sudden gust of wind brought her to her feet, and she quickly jumped up and closed the window. She was still chuckling aloud as she checked her look in the mirror and exited the room. The emerald-green taffeta crinoline under her elegant dress rustled as she descended the stairs and made her way toward a poker table near a bar. The cowhands around the table shifted their attention from their cards to Mary. "You have any room for me, fellows?" she purred. The men quickly made a space for Mary, and she smiled indulgently at them as she took a seat. "It would appear I have more friends than fiddlers in hell," she chortled.

⸺◆⸺

The twenty-five-year-old lady gambler, better known to her competitors as Mary the Owl, purchased a stack of chips from the dealer and waited for the game to begin. Any hope her so-called friends had of winning a hand were dashed in no time. She had acquired her moniker because of her keen eyesight at the table. Few could beat her at five-card draw poker.

Mary was born in upstate New York in 1846. She was one of ten children and her family was quite poor. She left home at the age of sixteen because there wasn't enough to eat. For four years she worked at a convent in New York City, training to be a nurse, but she abandoned the profession when she realized she could never earn enough money to fully support herself. When she was twenty she moved to Chicago and became involved with a con man named Philip Cartwright.

Cartwright was a sophisticated charlatan who took Mary into his confidence and taught her the trade. He saw in Mary all a person had to have to be a successful con artist: nerves of steel, a powerful imagination, and the calculating mind of a gambler. Cartwright helped develop her natural talent for swindling, but she eventually outgrew his direction.

Mary was never satisfied working small-time bunko games; she aspired to be a part of a large scam that would make her financially independent. After three years with Cartwright, she set out on her own. The gambling table provided her with a plenty to live on, and the occasional big score gave her a little extra. In late 1869 Mary pulled off an elaborate con with two other accomplices: Jimmy "the Peep" Coates and John Burtin, known as "the Smiling One" because he was always grinning. The

Among the many gambling pastimes women enjoyed besides blackjack, chuck-a-luck, and faro was a Pottawatomie dice game. The craps-style game consisted of thirteen individual pieces cut from bone and tossed into a pan. It was a favorite of Native American women at the reservation near Mayetta, Kansas, shown in this photograph ca. 1936.
THE DENVER PUBLIC LIBRARY, WESTERN HISTORY COLLECTION, X-232697

three managed to sell fraudulent exclusive shipping rights to the Mississippi to a group of French investors. The job netted Mary more than a quarter of a million dollars.

Mary and her cohorts were not only exceptional swindlers, but excellent actors as well. Using makeup, costumes, and different accents, the three were able to assume various roles while keeping their true identities a secret. Hoping to take advantage of the wealthy gold mine owners in California, the group took their show west in 1871. While en route to the Gold Country, Mary conceived of a plan to separate the well-known banker William Chapman Ralston from his millions. The scheme turned out to be the West's greatest hoax. Upon arriving in San Francisco in mid-June 1871, Mary and her coconspirators went to work setting the stage for the con.

Ralston was renowned throughout the frontier and often referred to as "the Magician of San Francisco." He was dedicated to transforming the growing city into one of the world's corporate and cultural capitals. To that end he built factories and gigantic hotels and invested in steamships, telegraph companies, and silver miners in Nevada's Comstock. He was an ambitious, hopeful millionaire who saw unlimited possibilities in the development of the West.

Ralston created the Bank of California in 1863 and sold shares to twenty-two of the state's leading businessmen. He managed to generate $2 million in capital funds and eagerly set out to financially back projects he believed would substantially increase his investments.

Mary had read about Ralston in the newspapers and felt there was a way to take advantage of his enthusiastic (and what some of his critics called "bold") investment moves. She learned that the astute banker's main weakness was his fanatical belief in California's unlimited mineral wealth. San Francisco was in the midst of a second gold boom. The mines of 1849 had played out. There had been a slump in business, but new mines in Nevada brought the precious ore to San Francisco for shipment. The future looked bright, and people were talking about other minerals yet to be found.

There had been rumors of diamond fields in the hills of Northern California. Given the fact that so many riches had been found in the area, most believed in the possibility that there was an abundance of gems in the same location. Ralston was one of those believers. Mary the Owl knew this, and it became a major part of her plan.

Twenty minutes after Mary's accomplices had entered the bank dressed as prospectors, news of their diamond mine had reached Ralston. He leaped to his feet and demanded that the clerk who spoke with the miners find them and bring them to him at once. Still dressed in their costumes, Jimmy and John were waiting in their hotel room when the clerk arrived. "Mr. Ralston wants to see you both," he blurted out. "He's real excited about the diamonds."

"We ain't wanting to sell any of our diamonds," John answered. "Being as we have enough to eat on, we want to keep them until we bring in a real fortune."

"Mr. Ralston doesn't want to buy your diamonds," the clerk assured them. "He just wants to meet you and talk to you."

The two accompanied the clerk to the bank. Ralston was all smiles and cordiality. The con men were cautious and pretended to be dumb. They admitted they had found the diamonds in the mountains, but did not say where because they wanted to make a big haul first. Ralston was amused at their seeming naiveté. The banker was not out to steal anything from anybody. He envisioned a great diamond mine that would make California the center of the diamond trade and run the English and their African mines out of the market.

"Now, gentlemen," Ralston said to the two, "you have discovered something big for you. You must realize that to develop this field will take millions. I am ready to advance you, say, $50,000 for an option to buy 70 percent of your interest. Your 25 percent will make you each fabulously rich."

The two prospectors didn't act like they were impressed. "Maybe we ain't smart," John said, "but we figure as how we can go out there and pick up a couple of million dollars in diamonds . . . that'll be enough. Then we don't care who knows about our field."

That was the one thing Ralston feared. The last thing he wanted was this amazing find to be turned loose on the market. He knew the Old West, and he knew the bloodspilling this would cause. He knew also that in the end there would be no great diamond development for the Californians. But as he pushed his offer to buy an option, he ran into a peculiar refusal. Neither would say yes or no. Finally John said, "I'll allow it if my sister can speak with you. She's a schoolteacher and mighty smart. She can understand about this money thing."

At that moment Mary stepped into the convincing scene being performed in Ralston's office. She was adorned in a black dress, her hair had been grayed around the edges, and she was wearing glasses and makeup. She looked like a middle-aged schoolteacher. By the end of her conversation with Ralston, he had raised his offer to $100,000 and she had accepted.

Ralston entered into the agreement with the predictable stipulations. Before the money could be paid, he told them, he would have to have assurance there was a diamond mine where the two men claimed.

"Naturally, Mr. Ralston," Mary said sweetly. "I would not permit my brother to take a penny from you unless he can prove to you there is a diamond mine." Ralston was impressed with the honesty and forthright manner of the sister. He and two friends were taken to the spot where the prospectors claimed they had found the diamonds. A part of the way they were blindfolded. Mary had insisted on it, as she said, "to protect the interests of my brother and his friend."

When the blindfold was taken off, Ralston and his friends were on the side of a foothill of the mountains. What they found dispelled any doubts Ralston might have had. They didn't have to dig long until they brought up diamonds by the handful.

This settled the matter for Ralston. When he got back to San Francisco, he sent a cable to his friend and former partner, Asbury Harpending, in London. Harpending was preoccupied with his own business ventures and initially glossed over the matter. Once out of her costume, Mary let the word get out about the diamond find, and the news reached one of Harpending's British associates. He warned Harpending not to take the report lightly, as America was a new and rich country and anything was possible there.

Ralston continued sending cables to Harpending in hopes that he would set aside all other ventures and concentrate on the diamonds. Harpending eventually did and then made way for California. After Harpending arrived he spoke with the two prospectors, checked their statements, and believed their story to be genuine. He made one requirement: The diamonds were to be examined by an expert at Tiffany's in New York. This prompted Mary to join in the discussion. Harpending was as impressed as Ralston with her honesty and levelheaded way of protecting her brother. She agreed that the diamonds should be examined by an expert.

Harpending took the gems to New York, where he had Mr. Tiffany and his experts examine the stones. They pronounced the diamonds of rare value, worth easily $150,000. By this time the news of the diamond field had reached New York City. It caused a market stampede for shares of the new mining company, even though no company had yet been organized.

Harpending was not satisfied with the opinion of the experts at Tiffany's, however. He insisted that a diamond expert from New York make a survey of the alleged diamond field. Mary again appeared for her brother. She was sweet but firm in her contention that the time had come for Ralston and the big boys to talk real money. After all, she argued, her dear brother was turning over to them a fortune of untold proportions and nothing had been said about what he and his friend were to get.

The gifted con woman played her hand shrewdly. She approved of the diamond field being seen by an expert, but before her brother agreed to any act that would disclose his secrets, an arrangement had to be reached first on how much money he was to get.

The Tiffany report had sent the hopes of Ralston and Harpending to soaring heights. They were easy suckers for Mary's wiles. When she left the bank, she had secured $200,000 cash with $800,000 put in escrow, to be paid when the expert agreed that her brother had found the world's largest diamond mine. Ralston and Harpending felt that they were taking no chances. They had $150,000 in diamonds as security for the $200,000, and if the diamond expert declared the find to be what they expected, the additional $800,000 would be a minor amount in comparison.

Ralston, Harpending, the gem expert, Jimmy, and John went to the diamond field. This time there were no blindfolds. The gem expert started his examination immediately upon arrival at the field. Everywhere he turned he found diamonds, and this time there were sapphires and opals at the location as well. The expert declared the field to be one of the greatest in the world and estimated it to be worth countless millions.

The expert and the investors were so excited about the discovery that they did not stop to consider two very important points: One, opals and sapphires are not a part of a diamond bed; and two, there were lapidary tool marks on many of the diamonds. Not only were those facts overlooked, but the expert, who was supposed to know diamonds, said they were of the finest quality.

The expert's report clinched the deal for Ralston and Harpending, and they filed claims for the area. The $800,000 held in escrow at the bank was released to Mary and her accomplices. The three then quickly left the state.

The positive report by the diamond expert rocked the financial world, and news of the find was a newspaper sensation. Ralston and Harpending organized a company and were instantly flooded with requests to buy stock. The popular businessmen allowed only a handful to invest a total of $2 million each. Any plans they had for the funds that were to be made off the diamond field were short lived. One week after Ralston and Harpending established their company and gathered the capital needed to start mining, the truth about the diamond field was discovered. A young engineer and friend of Ralston's was passing the diamond claim and stopped to investigate. He inspected a few of the gems scattered about and noticed they had been wedged in the crevices. Additionally, all had the marks of a lapidary tool—marks that raw diamonds do not possess.

When the engineer returned to San Francisco, he showed the cut diamonds to Ralston and Harpending. The two men were stunned at the discovery. Although they were embarrassed that they had fallen for the scam, they went public with information about the fraud and returned all the investors' money. Four years after the incident, due to lack of funds, Ralston was forced to close the doors of the bank he had founded. Harpending left the business world as well and turned his attention to writing. In 1877 he penned a book on the outrageous con entitled *The Great Diamond Hoax*. In the book he defended his reputation against those who suspected he aided the con artists in their work. Authorities speculated that he bribed the diamond expert who authenticated the claim.

The executioners of the million-dollar swindle had gone their separate ways. John Burtin lost all his money gambling and was arrested in Cleveland for defrauding a widow out of her life savings. Jimmy Coates used his winnings to purchase a farm in Georgia. Mary Hamlin traveled to London and made her home in the country for ten years. In 1882 she returned to New York City, where she lived out the remainder of her days in luxury. She died in 1899 of natural causes.

Ella Watson

Wyoming Cattle Baroness

"The lynching of Postmaster Averill and his wife on the Sweetwater Sunday night occurred about as reported in this paper yesterday morning. A Carbon County deputy Sheriff has laid himself liable to trouble by invading Fremont County with an armed posse and threatening to arrest the lynchers."

CHEYENNE DAILY LEADER, JULY 24, 1889

As Ella "Kate" Watson sashayed down the crude staircase of the Rawlins, Wyoming, saloon and brothel where she worked, she inspected the potential customers in the smoke-filled bar. Eager cowboys eyed her hourglass form as she brushed by them. They sniffed the air after her, breathing in the scent of jasmine she left behind. Kate looked past the scruffy wranglers vying for her attention and fixed her gaze on a tall, lean, well-dressed man sitting alone at a table, drinking.

"I'm Kate," she cooed to the handsome gentlemen as she walked up to him. "Would you like some company?"

The man nodded, smoothed down his mustache, and slammed down another shot of whiskey. "Jim Averill. I'm pleased to meet you."

Kate had seen Jim in the saloon before. He wasn't like any of the other men who frequented the bordellos where she worked. Jim was a civil engineer and a gifted writer who had served in the army. His entrepreneurial spirit had driven him west to make his fortune in whatever venture presented itself. When Kate and Jim met on February 24, 1886, Jim was ranching. He owned a small spread along the Sweetwater River where the Rawlins-Lander stage line crossed the Oregon Trail. The supply store he had opened at the stage stop was very profitable. He sold groceries, whiskey, and other items cowboys needed.

Kate had long since given up hope of ever meeting an accomplished man like Jim. She was the daughter of a wealthy farmer in Smith County,

Kansas, and was accustomed to fine things. In her teens she married a man who promised to provide her with the lifestyle in which she was raised, but the marriage ended when she found him with another woman. By the time she was twenty, Kate was divorced and earning a living as a prostitute in Wyoming. She preferred to work at houses in cow towns rather than burgs near army outposts because cowboys paid better.

Kate was too ambitious to remain a common percentage girl. She was always looking for new opportunities—opportunities that would lead her to a position of wealth and power. Jim possessed the same drive, and Kate fell in love with him. After the two enjoyed a few days of pleasure, Jim rode back to his ranch. Kate was left alone in her room at the brothel, praying he would return her feelings. But Jim had other things on his mind for the time being.

The years between 1887 and 1892 were a time of tension between big ranchers and small operators like Jim. Larger ranchers used vast areas of government land for grazing their cattle, yet they actually owned only small parcels of land on which to build their homes. Small ranchers could use only land that they owned to graze their cattle. The power in Wyoming counties naturally rested with the big ranchers who operated the Wyoming Stock Growers Association and who had substantial backing in the territorial legislature. Successful Jim Averill was a thorn in the association's side, and he made its secret hit list after refusing to vacate his property and give up his land. He further fueled the rift when he agreed to become the spokesperson for the smaller ranching operations.

Jim brought the small rancher's case into the public eye by writing numerous letters to the editors of Casper newspapers. He also used other tactics, such as forcing his opponents to prove their claim to the lands on which their ranches were located.

Kate had heard about the war between large ranch owners and small homesteaders. Not a night went by that there wasn't a saloon fight over who had rights to various pieces of land. Kate's business decreased as the trouble escalated. Her clients were preoccupied with the range war.

In May 1886 Kate was staring out her window, drinking in the sun, when the barkeep handed her a letter from Jim. A broad smile filled her face as she carefully opened the neatly penned, purple-prose letter. "My dearest Kate, I need you here with me. Please say you'll come. Always,

Jim." Kate was thrilled. This was proof that Jim Averill had feelings for her. She sent word back to Jim that she was on her way and set her sights on the two of them getting married and amassing a cattle fortune.

Kate arrived at Jim's homestead in late spring 1886. The cabin and general store on his property were rustic, but they were set against the backdrop of rolling hills and a sparkling river. The range that spread out before them was dotted with cattle. Jim had a good start on a herd, and Kate was awash with enthusiasm, imagining the possibilities for their future.

Jim had his mind on the future as well. His position as spokesperson for the small ranchers served as the perfect entrée into politics. He had become postmaster and justice of the peace for his district, and he believed these new positions would bring him credibility with the territorial legislature. He could state his case for homesteaders and force the government to enact laws to protect the landowners in Sweetwater Valley. Jim wanted one of those landowners to be Kate. Any idea she had about setting up house with him was quickly extinguished. Jim moved Kate onto her own ranch—a piece of land he had filed for under the Homestead Act using Kate's name.

It didn't take long for Jim to convince Kate that two homesteads meant the chance for financial security. According to the Homestead Act, the two merely had to live on the land for five years and it would then belong to them. Jim promised to marry Kate when they had made final proof on their homesteads. Kate agreed and moved her things into the ranch house Jim had built for her, a log structure with a pale green door and shutters to match.

Kate proved to be a drawing card at Jim's store. Men would come from miles around just to look at her. Women were revered in Wyoming. The October 12, 1917, edition of the *Wyoming State Journal* reported that in Wyoming there was one woman for every one hundred men. Jim installed a bar in the back of his establishment, and it was frequented by cowhands from every big and small ranch in the valley.

Jim considered Kate to be a good investment. Kate was eager to please him, not only because she loved Jim, but because she loved money and everything that went along with it.

Cattle Kate was hanged for rustling cattle and defying the Wyoming Stock Growers Association.

Jim and his men rounded up range strays, marked them with Jim's own brand, and shipped them off to eastern markets. Kate and Jim quickly became two of the richest ranchers in the area. Jim bought expensive clothes, wore gold cufflinks and watch chains, and even sent away for imported cigars. He took Kate on shopping trips to Denver, where she bought new dresses by the dozen. All the while Jim kept up his barrage against the Wyoming Stock Growers Association. Members of the association, upset with Jim's ever-increasing wealth, continued to issue warnings to him to vacate his property or be killed. Jim refused to be scared off.

Jim became preoccupied with planning the demise of the association and started to ignore Kate. In retaliation Kate kept company with some of the cowboys who came into the store. She accepted stolen cattle from the men in return for her favors, thus earning her the nickname "Cattle Kate." Stories soon spread that stolen yearlings could be found among Kate's cattle. If they were not in her pasture, it was because she was passing them on to Jim, some alleged.

The Wyoming Stock Growers Association accused Jim of being the head of a gigantic rustling ring. Its leaders produced no evidence that he was a rustler, but the association was intent on blackening his reputation and driving him out of the valley.

Jim was always quick to come to Kate's defense. He didn't believe the rumors he felt were perpetrated by the association. He chose instead to believe that Kate had bought the yearlings outright with money he had given her. In early July 1889 an article championing both Jim and Kate's actions appeared in the newspaper *Bill Barlow's Budget*. Jim's hired hands later told historians that he was humiliated by the piece. It read: "Averill is not a rustler, and while his woman, Watson did have stolen stock in her possession it is a fact that she, herself, did not steal, or illegally brand a single calf. She bought them as any other prostitute buys."

Kate and Jim never discussed the stolen cattle. The pair continued on as though the entire event had never happened. Jim's loyalty to Kate in spite of her infidelity caused her to feel more for him. She vowed to stand by him forever and help him win his fight against the Wyoming Stock Growers Association.

On July 20, 1889, a hot sun beat down on the ranch of cattle king Albert J. Bothwell. Members of the association had converged at his place for an emergency meeting. Albert convinced the members that to maintain control of the range, they needed to take immediate action against their most staunch opponents, Jim Averill and Kate Watson. He believed if those two were out of the way, the other landowners wouldn't dare stay on.

The association agreed to ride out to Jim's place that afternoon and deliver one last ultimatum to the couple. They would give them a choice between leaving Sweetwater Valley while they still had their health or being forcibly ejected. The men knew Jim was a proud, fearless man who would choose the latter. Thus Albert threw a pair of ropes over his saddle and led the party on its way.

Meanwhile, Kate strutted proudly over the flower-covered hillside near her ranch, stopping occasionally to admire the beaded moccasins she had just bought from the Shoshone Indians encamped by the river. Ranch hands John DeCorey and Gene Crowder were with her when the association members rode quickly past them. No words were exchanged.

When Kate, Crowder, and DeCorey reached her cabin, they found the association men waiting for them. Albert leveled his gun at the three while one of the other men took down the gate around Kate's cattle and drove them out to the pasture.

"Get in the wagon, Kate," Albert demanded.

"Where we going?" Kate asked.

"Rawlins," he said with a wry smile.

Kate studied the faces of the angry men. "I'll need to change first. I can't go to Rawlins looking like this," she told them.

"Get in the wagon now or I'll throw a rope around you and drag you the whole way!" Albert barked.

"What have you done with Jim?" Kate asked.

"Nothing . . . yet," Albert laughed.

Kate climbed into the wagon, and the group started for Jim's place. They caught up with Jim as he was hitching a team to drive to Casper for supplies and told him they had a warrant for his arrest. When he asked to see it, they patted their rifles and told him the guns were warrant enough.

They made him get in the wagon with Kate and then drove off in the direction of Independence Rock.

Kate tried to move close to Jim, but Albert wouldn't allow it. The association members drove their horses to Spring Creek Canyon. Frank Buchanan, one of Jim's ranch hands, followed along behind the party, careful to keep a safe distance back and out of sight.

Spring Creek Canyon was dry, and the creek bed was clogged with high brush and gigantic boulders. Frank stepped off his horse and continued up the canyon on foot. Using the boulders and brush for cover, he advanced until he caught sight of the lynch party and its victims. Lariats had been thrown over the limb of a scrub pine that projected out over the floor of the canyon from a limestone ledge. Frank opened fire on the mob, and they began shooting back. Seriously outnumbered, Frank decided to start out for Casper to get the sheriff.

"You're going to hang us, are you?" Kate snapped.

"Maybe we'll drown you," Albert huffed.

Kate looked down at the shallow river below and chuckled. "Hell, there ain't enough water in there to give you boys a bath," she quipped.

Albert gave the noose a hard tug. The bough above him bent under the strain. "How much you weigh, Cattle Kate?" he asked.

"You want to hold me in your lap and find out?" she snorted. "Are you gents trying to make yourselves a rep? Are you respectable cow men ganging up and lynching poor little Kate?" she sneered. The barb of contempt bit into the conscience of her audience. Frowns deepened on tanned faces.

"I think the branch will do," Albert said.

A couple of association members led the wagon to the canyon ledge, yanked Jim over to the rope, and slipped the noose around his neck. "Don't worry, Kate. They aren't really going to hang us," Jim assured her.

Albert threw a rope around Kate's neck and jerked it tight. "You're wrong, Averill. You're both nothing but cattle thieves," he snarled.

Kate cursed Albert and called the other men cowards. She looked over at Jim and blinked away a tear. Jim nodded to her as the association members pushed the two off the wagon. The pair didn't fall far enough to break their necks; they strangled to death while the mob watched. The angry ranchers left the scene, each going in a different direction after vowing never to say a word about what they had done.

By the time Frank Buchanan returned to the site with the lawmen, Kate and Jim's lifeless bodies were swaying to and fro in the breeze. Unbeknownst to the association, Kate's ranch hand Gene Crowder had also followed the men to the canyon and witnessed the lynching. He came forward and told the sheriff what he had seen and heard. Warrants were issued, and news of the hangings spread quickly throughout the West.

Newspaper readers were outraged that anyone would hang a woman. The *Salt Lake Tribune* commented, "The men of Wyoming will not be proud of the fact that a woman—albeit unsexed and totally depraved—had been hanged within their territory. That is the poorest use that a woman can be put to." The *Cheyenne Daily Leader* had a different take on the hangings. "Let justice be done," the article read. "All resorts to lynch law are deplorable in a country governed by laws, but when the law shows itself powerless and inactive, when justice is lame and halting, when there is failure to convict on down-right proofs, it is not in the nature of enterprising western men to sit idly by and have their cattle stolen from under their very noses."

Two days after Kate and Jim were hanged, their bodies were cut down. Kate's father arrived in Rawlins to claim his daughter's body, telling newspaper reporters that the cattlemen who accused his child of rustling were liars. "She never branded a hoof or threw a rope," he insisted.

Six men were eventually arrested. Albert Bothwell was among them, but the legal process was a farce from the beginning. Rawlins authorities were in the pockets of the association, and the six defendants were permitted to sign one another's bail bonds. The witnesses against the guilty association members, including Frank Buchanan, began to disappear one by one. By the time the trial began, there was no one left to testify against the mob, and the defendants were discharged.

Jim's ranch house and store were torn down, and the lumber was carted away to be used a second time. Cattle Kate's small cabin was sold at auction for $14.19. The purchaser was Albert Bothwell. He had the building dragged to his ranch, where he used it for an icehouse.

A curious Rawlins citizen who visited the site where the couple was hanged retrieved the moccasins Kate had on when she died. They had fallen off her feet during the hanging. The moccasins are now on display at the Wyoming State Museum.

Kate and Jim were laid to rest in shallow graves on Jim's land. A few years later their remains were moved to a cemetery in Casper.

Rose Ellis

Last of the Old West Madams

"There never was a more beautiful person in the world. She lived to help children, filling their Christmas stockings with nickels and dimes, buying gifts, and donating Yuletide trees for her girls and the poor."
MADAM TEXAS TOMMY'S CHAUFFEUR, AUGUST 11, 1982

The light from a full October moon filtered through the open window beside Rose Ellis's bed. The eighty-four-year-old woman stared thoughtfully into the night sky, then closed her eyes in a half-hearted attempt to block out the peaceful image. Tears rolled off her tormented face onto the pillow underneath her head. The evening was calm and still, but her emotions were not. The sheets and blankets that once neatly covered her bed were crumpled, and some were lying on the floor. Rose was restless, troubled. "Don't worry," she whispered to herself, "I know what must be done."

The Belmont Rest Home in San Francisco, where Rose had just moved, was a sparsely decorated, sterile environment—a stark contrast to the parlor houses she had furnished and managed in her younger years. Rose's eighty-two-year-old sister, Buena, was lying in a bed a few feet away from her. Buena had lived with Rose her entire life. She wasn't any more accustomed to her homogenized surroundings than Rose, but she had managed to fall asleep. Rose was grateful for that. Buena was developmentally disabled and seemed least harassed by the challenges of life when she slept.

As Rose watched her sister's slow, steady breathing she thought back to the promise she had made her father to take care of Buena. On November 11, 1918, news that the Ellis girls' father had died sent Buena into shock. Doctors performed a lobotomy on the distressed woman, which left her brain damaged. Rose pledged to care for her only living relative for the rest of her life.

Old age, lack of funds, and limited options forced Rose to commit herself and Buena to the rest home. Although it was not an ideal situation, Rose was resigned to the living conditions. When doctors informed her that she had very little time to live, she decided to reevaluate the arrangement. The alternative she arrived at was extreme but necessary. It weighed heavily on her heart.

Lifting herself out of her bed, Rose shuffled over to a large bureau and slowly opened the top drawer. She removed a .38 caliber, nickel-plated revolver hidden under a stack of camisoles. She opened the gun and loaded two bullets into the chamber.

Taking a deep breath, she made her way to Buena's bed, knelt down, and kissed her on the cheek. Using all the strength in both her aged hands, she pulled the hammer back and held the weapon to her sister's ear. A shot rang out and Buena was gone.

Tears streamed down Rose's face as she cocked the gun again and pressed it to her own temple. "See you soon, my darling sister," she whispered to Buena's lifeless form. The final shot was fired. Rose fell in a heap on the floor, the smoking gun still clutched in her hand.

Little is known about Rose's early life. Much of the information on hand at the Searls Historical Library in Nevada City, California, was acquired from one of Rose's longtime friends, a native historian who worked for the local railroad and assisted Rose with her baggage and transportation to and from her parlor house.

Rose Aline Ellis was born in 1878. Her father was a wealthy South Dakota miner. Her mother died when Rose and her sister were very young. The father doted on his daughters, giving them every advantage he could afford. In 1910, after learning about the business opportunities on the West Coast, he moved his family to San Francisco. He hoped to earn enough to secure a future for his daughters. Rose was forty years old when he died.

Left with the awesome responsibility of caring for her handicapped sister, Rose decided to pursue a career in the oldest profession in the world. Prostitution was a lucrative business. Rose was aware of how well the madams in the area did and believed that was the only job that would bring in the funds needed to help Buena. Rose managed parlor houses up and down the Bay Area's red-light district from 1918 to 1929.

Texas Tommy, aka Rose Ellis, poses with her dog in 1923.

The economy was suffering throughout the United States in 1930. There were a few businesses that continued to revel in prosperity, one of which was prostitution. After eleven years of working for various brothel owners, Rose decided to go into the prostitution business on her own. She opened her first house in Nevada County. The area boasted the richest gold mine in the state. Nevada City, where her house was located, was the third-largest city in California. Thousands of ambitious miners had descended upon the spot to extract tons of gold ore from the rich earth.

Rose called her house the Golden Gate Amusement Company. Patrons of the three-story yellow house on Spring Street referred to the vivacious madam as Texas Tommy. To accommodate three shifts of men working in the mines, she kept her doors open twenty-four hours a day.

Rose used the considerable profits from the house to purchase a grand nightclub that catered to both men and women. It was a fashionable saloon with sparkling chandeliers, red velvet drapes, a large stage, and an orchestra pit complete with instruments. Champagne flowed from fountains and the finest food was served. Six weeks after the Heidelberg Club opened, the building caught fire and burned to the ground. Arson was suspected, but local authorities could not find the culprit. Nevada County residents speculated that a jealous housewife torched the brothel, but no proof of that ever materialized.

Once the ashes had been swept away, Rose's attention shifted solely to her brothel. Her house was always busy, especially on payday—so much so that she had to send for extra entertainers to come in and help. Rose charged clients $2.50 for the company of one of her girls. Many of the ladies made as much as $50 a night. Rose received 20 percent of their earnings.

Madam Tommy is reported to have been quite generous with the wealth she acquired. Not only did she shower Buena with beautiful clothes and gifts, she also contributed funds to help support poor and hungry children. Whenever a miner died from an on-the-job injury, a wagonload of groceries and firewood would mysteriously appear on the widow's doorstep. Although she never admitted it, townspeople agreed that Texas Tommy was the source of the supplies.

Madam Tommy always appeared in public immaculately dressed. Her auburn hair was nicely styled and more often than not adorned with a rose. She expected the girls that worked for her to follow her example in keeping a neat and orderly appearance. She believed people treated you with respect if you looked like you respected yourself. On those rare occasions when Rose was treated rudely, she would scold the offender for his actions and warn him to "never let it happen again."

A teller at the Nevada County bank refused to cash a dividend check Rose and Buena had received from one of her father's mines in the Dakotas. The banker's actions so enraged the madam that she stormed out of the establishment vowing to never do business there again. When she finally did get the check cashed (at an out-of-town bank), she used the money to throw a party in every saloon in town and persuaded all those in attendance to consider ending their association with the Nevada County bank.

Those close to Texas Tommy noted that she was an extravagant spender. It was not uncommon for her to purchase breakfast for her girls and their overnight guests, rent out entire hotels for wild celebrations, buy expensive presents for children in the neighborhood, and treat railroad baggage handlers to a night on the town. Nevada County, California, historian and railroad employee Bob Paine recalled one such night during an interview he did with the *Independent* newspaper in Nevada City, California, on October 14, 1981:

> *One night in 1936—in the line of official duties of course . . . I went to collect the weekly passenger fares. Texas suggested we paint the town a little bit red. She opened a drawer in her office. I had never seen so much money in my life: $5, $10, and $20 bills to overflowing. On top of the whole pile was a small pearl handled pistol. Texas lifted her satin skirt and stuffed her voluminous bloomers with bills of every denomination and away we went to every saloon in Nevada County.*

Madam Tommy's Golden Gate Amusement Company remained in operation until 1942, when the US Army forced her to close her doors. Because the country was at war, soldiers were required to wear their uniforms at all times. The order made secret visits to Tommy's place difficult. Off-duty soldiers from a nearby army post were frequently caught at the parlor house. They were severely reprimanded and told to stay away from the house. The soldiers devised a plan to change into mechanics' overalls and slip in undetected. After a sharp-eyed reporter at the local newspaper exposed the activity, the military and law enforcement moved in and shut the business down.

Madam Tommy and her sister returned to the Bay Area in 1943. Rose took care of Buena as long as she was able. Once Rose's health began to decline, she moved them both into a nursing home. On April 26, 1962, news of the tragic demise of the kindhearted madam and her sister made the front page of the *San Francisco Chronicle*: "She was driven by an undying devotion to her sister. . . . Even in death Texas Tommy had class and courage. So let's close this sad story with Jesus' admonishment in his Sermon on the Mount. 'Let he who is without sin cast the first stone.'"

Bibliography

General Sources

Aikman, Duncan. *Calamity Jane and the Lady Wildcats*. Lincoln: University of Nebraska Press, 1927.

Anonymous. *The Denver Red Book. A Reliable Directory of the Pleasure Resorts of Denver*. Denver, CO, 1892.

Ball, Eve. *The Women Who Made the West*. New York: Avon Books, 1980.

Barry, Kathleen. *The Prostitution of Sexuality*. New York: New York University Press, 1995.

Bettmann, Otto. *The Good Old Days—They Were Terrible!* New York: Random House, 1974.

Brown, Dee. *The Gentle Tamers: Women of the Old West*. Lincoln: University of Nebraska Press, 1958.

Churchill, C. M. *The Social Evil*. San Francisco: Bancroft Press, 1872.

Convis, Charles. *Gamblers*. Carson City, NV: Pioneer Press, 2000.

Dary, David. *Seeking Pleasure in the Old West*. New York: Alfred A. Knopf, 1995.

Gentry, Curt. *The Madams of San Francisco*. Garden City, NY: Doubleday & Company, 1964.

Hoyles, Edward. *Hoyles Game: The Standard Authority*. New York: Excelsior Publishing House, 1887.

Kelly, Bill. *Gamblers of the Old West*. Las Vegas: B&F Enterprises, 1995.

Nash, Robert Jay. *Encyclopedia of Western Lawmen & Outlaws*. New York: Paragon House, 1989.

Neil, Kagen. *The Gamblers of the Old West*. Richmond, VA: Time-Life Books, 1996.

Ringdal, Nils Johan. *Love for Sale: A World History of Prostitution*. Translated by Richard Daly. New York: Grove Press, 2003.

Seagraves, Anne. *Soiled Doves: Prostitution in the Early West*. Hayden, ID: Wesanne Publications, 1994.

Ward, Geoffrey C., and Dayton Duncan. *The West: An Illustrated History*. Boston: Little Brown & Company, 1996.

Gertrudis Maria Barceló

Briggs, Walter. "The Lady They Called La Tules." *New Mexico Magazine*, Spring 1927.

Chavez, Fray A. "Don Tules, Her Fame and Her Funeral." *El Palacio* 57, no. 8 (August 1959).

Horgan, Paul. *The Centuries of Santa Fe.* Albuquerque: University of New Mexico Press, 1956.

Peavy, Linda, and Ursula Smith. *Pioneer Women: The Lives of Women on the Frontier.* Norman: University of Oklahoma Press, 1998.

Julia Bulette

Hegne, Barbara. *Harlots, Hurdies & Spirited Women of Virginia City, Nevada.* Medford, OR: FreeStyle Graphics, 2001.

Janesville Gazette. Janesville, WI. June 9, 1868.

Reno Gazette. Reno, NV. November 9, 1955.

Williams, George III. *The Red Light Ladies of Virginia City, Nevada.* Carson City, NV: Tree by the River Publishing. 1984.

Martha Jane Canary

Aikman, Duncan. *Calamity Jane and the Lady Wildcats.* Lincoln: University of Nebraska Press, 1927.

Black Hills Daily Times. Deadwood, SD. July 15, 1876.

Black Hills Daily Times. Deadwood, SD. February 8, 1879.

DuFran, Dora. *Low Down on Calamity Jane.* Deadwood, SD: Helen Rezatto, 1981.

Farber, Doris. *Calamity Jane: Her Life and Her Legend.* Boston: Houghton Mifflin, 1992.

Rezatto, Helen. *Vignettes of Pioneers and Notables.* Northbrook, IL: North Plains Press, 1980.

Belle Ryan Cora

Bancroft, Hubert. *El Dorado and the Beautiful Bad.* Los Angeles: Historic Record Company, 1924.

Jolly, Michelle. "Sex, Vigilantism, and San Francisco in 1856." *Early Cities of the Americas* 3, no. 4 (July 2003). Accessed July 17, 2014. www.common-place.org/vol-03/no-04/san-francisco.

Richards, Rand. *Historic San Francisco.* San Francisco: Heritage House Publishing, 1991.

Florence Mabel Dedrick

Bell, Ernest A. *Fighting the Traffic in Young Girls or War on the White Slave Trade.* Chicago: Salvation Army Publication, 1910.

Dedrick, Florence Mabel. *For God's Sake Do Something.* Chicago: Salvation Army Publication, 1910.

Lottie Deno

Harold, Lloyd J. *Southwest New Mexico History.* Deming, NM: Historical Society Publishing, 1971.

Hunter, Marvin J. *The Story of Lottie Deno: Her Life and Times.* Santa Fe: The 4 Hunters Publishing, 1959.

Rose, Cynthia. "Deno, Lottie," Handbook of Texas Online. Accessed August 1, 2014. www.tshaonline.org/handbook/online/articles/fde59.

Rose, Cynthia. *Lottie Deno: Gambling Queen of Hearts.* Santa Fe: Clear Light Publishers, 1994.

Stanley, F. *The Deming, New Mexico Story.* Deming, NM: Historical Society Publishing, 1962.

Eleanora Dumont

Aikman, Duncan. *Madam Mustache & Other Gaming Ladies.* New York: Henry Holt & Company, 1927.

Brown, Dee. *The Gentle Tamers: Women of the Old Wild West.* Lincoln: University of Nebraska Press, 1958.

Chartier, J., and Chris Enss. *With Great Hope: Women of the California Gold Rush.* Guilford, CT: Globe Pequot Press, 2000.

Drago, Harry S. *Notorious Ladies of the Frontier.* New York: Ballantine Books, 1972.

Johnson, Russ, and Ann Johnson. *The Ghost Town of Bodie.* Bishop, CA: Sierra Media, 1967.

Paine, Bob. "Madame Moustache—A Glimpse of History." *The Mountain Messenger*, December 9, 1982.

Parkhill, Forbes. *The Wildest of the West.* New York: Henry Holt & Company, 1951.

Perkins, William. *Memoirs of William Perkins.* Berkley, CA: Perkins Books, 1893.

Ross, Edward A. *Madam Mustache: Pioneer of the Parlor House Circuit.* Cleveland, OH: Quirk Books, 1981.

Seagraves, Anne. *Women of the Sierra*. Lakeport, CA: Wesanne Enterprises, 1990.

Zauner, Phyllis. *Those Spirited Women of the Early West*. Sonoma, CA: Zanel Publications, 1994.

Rose Ellis

Janicott, Michelle. *Ladies of the Night*. Nevada City, CA: Nevada County Historical Society, 1994.

"Texas Tommy—Was She a Saint or a Sinner?" *Independent*, Nevada City, CA, August 11, 1982.

"Whorehouses in the West." *Independent*, Nevada City, CA, October 14, 1981.

Mary Hamlin

Conrow, Robert. *The Great Diamond Hoax and Other True Tales*. Boulder, CO: Johnson Books, 1983.

Harpending, Asbury. *The Great Diamond Hoax*. London, UK: Fredonia Books, 1877.

Morgan, Carl H. "Diamond Mary and the Million Dollar Swindle." *Real West Magazine*, April 1958.

Tilton, Cecil G. *William Chapman Ralston: Courageous Builder*. Costa Mesa, CA: Christopher Publishing House, 1935.

Wilkens, James. *The Great Diamond Hoax and Other Great Stirring Incidents in the Life of Asbury Harpending*. Boston: James H. Barry Publishing, 1915.

Jessie Hayman

Allen, Robert S. *Jessie Hayman: San Francisco's Other Fire*. New York: Vanguard Press, 1947.

Caen, Herb. *Only in San Francisco*. New York: Doubleday & Company, 1960.

The Laws of the Town of San Francisco. San Marino, CA: The Huntington Library, 1947.

Kate Horony

Boyer, Glenn. *Who Was Big Nose Kate? Vol. 1 of Wyatt Earp: Family, Friends & Foes*. Rodeo, NM: Historical Research Associates, 1997.

Chartier, Joann, and Chris Enss. *Love Untamed: Romances of the Old West*. Guilford, CT: Globe Pequot Press, 2002.

Coleman, Jane C. *Doc Holliday's Woman*. Clayton, Victoria, Australia: Warner Books, 1995.

Fiske, Jack. *Big Nose Kate*. Tombstone, AZ: Big Nose Kate's Saloon Publishing, 1997.

Jahns, Pat. *The Frontier World of Doc Holliday*. New York: Indian Head Books, 1957.

Robinson, Olivia. *She Did It Her Way*. New York: Putnam Press, 1946.

Alice Ivers

Aikman, Duncan. *Calamity Jane and the Lady Wildcats*. Lincoln: University of Nebraska Press, 1927.

Fielder, Mildred. *Poker Alice*. Deadwood, SD: Centennial Distributors, 1978.

"Long Cigar—Trademark of Poker Alice." *Lead Daily Call*, Lead, SD, July 28, 1967.

Mezulla, Fred, and Jo Mezulla. *Outlaw Albums*. Denver: A. D. Hirschfeld Press, 1966.

"Poker Alice Tubbs Found Gold Plentiful in Deadwood Gulch at the Town Gambling Tables." *Deadwood Pioneer Times*, July 28, 1961.

Rezatto, Helen. *Tales of the Black Hills*. Rapid City, SD: Fenwyn Press, 1989.

Kitty LeRoy

Black Hills Daily Times. Deadwood, SD. May 19, 1877.

Black Hills Daily Times. Deadwood, SD. June 11, 1877.

Black Hills Daily Times. Deadwood, SD. December 7, 1877.

Black Hills Daily Times. Deadwood, SD. January 7, 1878.

Black Hills Daily Times. Deadwood, SD. February 28, 1878.

Black Hills Daily Times. Deadwood, SD. November 21, 1881.

Rezatto, Helen. *Vignettes of Pioneers and Notables*. Northbrook, IL: North Plains Press, 1980.

Schell, Herbert S., and John E. Miller. *History of South Dakota*. Spearfish: South Dakota State Historical Society Press, 2004.

Madam Harriet

The Union News. Nevada County, CA. August 12, 1852.

Laura Bell McDaniel

Colorado City Iris. Colorado City, CO. May 7, 1909.

Colorado Springs Weekly Gazette. Colorado Springs, CO. April 30, 1903.

MacKell, Jan. *Brothels, Bordellos, & Bad Girls.* Albuquerque: University of New Mexico, 2004.

Salida Semi-Weekly Mail. Salida, CO. May 20, 1887.

Rosa May

Brown, Dee. *The Gentle Tamers: Women of the Old Wild West.* Lincoln: University of Nebraska Press, 1958.

Johnson, Russ, and Anne, Johnson. *The Ghost Town of Bodie.* Bishop, CA: Sierra Media, 1967.

Williams, George III. *The Red Light Ladies of Virginia City, Nevada.* Carson City, NV: Tree by the River Publishing, 1979.

Williams, George. *Rosa May: The Search for a Mining Camp Legend.* Carson City, NV: Tree by the River Publishing, 1979.

Kate O'Leary

Horan, James D. *Across the Cimarron.* New York: Bonanza Books, 1956.

Rosa, Joseph, and Waldo Koop. *Rowdy Joe Lowe: Gambler with a Gun.* Norman: University of Oklahoma Press, 1989.

Vestal, Stanley. *Queen of the Cowtowns: Dodge City.* New York: Harper & Brothers, 1998.

Jessie Reeves and Cad Thompson

Hegne, Barbara. *Harlots, Hurdies & Spirited Women of Virginia City.* Medford, OR: FreeStyle Graphics, 2001.

Myers, Sandra L. *Westering Women and the Frontier Experience.* Albuquerque: University of New Mexico Press, 1982.

Selcer, Richard. *Hell's Half Acre.* Fort Worth: Texas Christian University Press, 1991.

Williams, George III. *The Red Light Ladies of Virginia City, Nevada.* Carson City, NV: Tree by the River Publishing, 1984.

Jennie Rogers

Bancroft, Caroline. *Six Racy Madams of Colorado.* Boulder, CO: Johnson Publishing Company, 1965.

"Mattie's House of Mirrors," Rocky Mountain Paranormal Research Society. Accessed August 1, 2014. www.rockymountainparanormal.com/matties.html.

Selcer, Richard. *Hell's Half Acre*. Fort Worth: Texas Christian University Press, 1991.

Wommack, Linda R. *Our Ladies of the Tenderloin: Colorado's Legends in Lace*. Caldwell, ID: Caxton Press, 2004.

Jenny Rowe

Levy, Joann. *They Saw the Elephant: Women in the California Gold Rush*. Hamden, CT: She String Press, 1990.

Prowse, Brad. "Girl Bandit of the Sierras." *Union*, Grass Valley, CA, March 31, 2001.

Smith, James. *San Francisco's Lost Landmarks*. Sanger, CA: Word Dancer Press, 2005.

Belle Siddons

Aikman, Duncan. *Calamity Jane and the Lady Wildcats*. Lincoln: University of Nebraska Press, 1927.

Hockett, William. "Boone May—Gunfighter of the Black Hills, 2002." Accessed August 1, 2014. www.bar-w.com/boonemay.html.

Lee, Bob. *Gold, Gals, Guns, Guts: A History of Deadwood*. Pierre: South Dakota Historical Society Press, 2004.

Parker, Watson. *Deadwood: The Golden Years*. Lincoln: University of Nebraska Press, 1981.

Mattie Silks

Braun, Matt. *Mattie Silks*. Fort Worth: Pinnacle Books, 1985.

Bunch, Joey. "Denver's 'Queen of the Night Life' Helped Make Cow Town a Roost for Soiled Doves." *Denver Post*, November 15, 2012. Accessed August 1, 2014. http://blogs.denverpost.com/library/2012/11/15/mattie-silks-queen-denver-nightlife-ruled-kingdom-grace-force/4782/

Goldstein, Phil. *The Seamy Side of Denver*. Denver: New Social Publishers, 1993.

Miller, Max. *Holladay Street*. New York: New American Library, 1962.

Wallenchinsky, David, and Irving Wallace. *The People's Almanac*. New York: Doubleday, 1975.

"Western Women." The Spell of the West. Accessed August 1, 2014.
www.jcs-group.com/oldwest/women.html.

Minnie Smith

Bancroft, Caroline. *Six Racy Madams of Colorado*. Boulder, CO: Johnson
Publishing Company, 1965.

Collier, Grant, and Joseph Collier. *Colorado Yesterday and Today*. Lake-
wood, CO: Collier Publishing, 2005.

Hegne, Barbara. *Harlots, Hurdies & Spirited Women of Virginia City*.
Medford, OR: FreeStyle Graphics, 2001.

MacKell, Jan. *Brothels, Bordellos and Bad Girls*. Albuquerque: University
of New Mexico Press, 2004.

Williams, George. *The Red Light Ladies of Virginia City, Nevada*. Carson
City, NV: Tree by the River Publishing, 1984.

Belle Starr

Aikman, Duncan. *Calamity Jane and the Lady Wildcats*. Lincoln: University of Nebraska Press, 1927.

Parkhill, Forbes. *The Wildest of the West*. New York: Henry Holt & Company, 1951.

Rau, M. *Belle of the West: The True Story of Belle Starr*. Charlotte, NC:
Morgan Reynolds Publishing, 2001.

Reiter, Joan S. *The Women*. Alexandria, VA: Time-Life Books, 1978.

Shirley, Glenn. *Belle Starr and Her Times*. Norman: University of Oklahoma Press, 1990.

Libby Thompson

Butler, Anne M. *Daughter of Joy, Sisters of Mercy*. Chicago: University of
Illinois, 1987.

Gesell, Laurence. *Saddle the Wild Wind: The Saga of Squirrel Tooth Alice
and Texas Billy Thompson*. Chandler, AZ: Coast Aire, 2001.

Rosen, Ruth. *The Lost Sisterhood: Prostitution in America, 1900–1918*.
Baltimore: Johns Hopkins University Press, 1983.

Tessie Wall

Barnhart, Jacqueline. *The Fair but Frail: Prostitution in San Francisco*.
Reno: University of Nevada Press, 1986.

Erickson, Bill. *San Francisco Streetwalkers*. San Francisco: Bangkok Publications, 1973.

Wilson, J. Stitt. *The Barbary Coast in a Barbarous Land*. Los Angeles: Socialist Party of California, 1913.

Josie Washburn

Evans, Max. *Madam Millie: Bordellos from Silver City to Ketchikan*. Albuquerque: University of New Mexico Press, 2002.

Walkowitz, Judith. *Prostitution and Victorian Society: Women, Class, and the State*. Cambridge: Cambridge University Press, 1982.

Washburn, Josie. *The Underworld Sewer: A Prostitute Reflects on Life in the Trade, 1871–1909*. Lincoln: University of Nebraska, 1909.

Ella Watson

Cheyenne Daily Leader. Cheyenne, WY. July 23, 1889.

Cheyenne Daily Leader. Cheyenne, WY. September 19, 1889.

Daily Boomerang. Laramie, WY. July 25, 1889.

Hufsmith, George W. *The Wyoming Lynching of Cattle Kate*. Glendo, WY: High Plains Press, 1993.

Wyoming State Journal. Cheyenne, WY. October 12, 1917.

Index

ABOUT THE AUTHOR

Chris Enss is a *New York Times* best-selling author who has been writing about women of the Old West for more than a dozen years. She has penned more than thirty published books on the subject. Her book *Object Matrimony: The Risky Business of Mail-Order Matchmaking on the Western Frontier* (Globe Pequot) won the Elmer Kelton Award for best nonfiction book of 2013. Another recent Enss title, *Sam Sixkiller: Frontier Cherokee Lawman* (also Globe Pequot), was named Outstanding Book on Oklahoma History by the Oklahoma Historical Society. Enss also has received the Spirit of the West Alive award, cosponsored by the *Wild West Gazette*, celebrating her efforts to keep the spirit of the Old West alive for future generations.